THE LITTLE BOOK OF
VALUES

Educating children to become thinking, confident, responsible and caring citizens

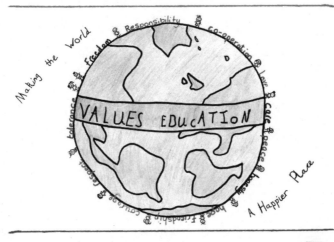

Julie Duckworth Edited by Ian Gilbert

Crown House Publishing Limited
www.crownhouse.co.uk – www.crownhousepublishing.com

First published by

Crown House Publishing Ltd
Crown Buildings, Bancyfelin, Carmarthen, Wales, SA33 5ND, UK
www.crownhouse.co.uk

and

Crown House Publishing Company LLC
6 Trowbridge Drive, Suite 5, Bethel, CT 06801, USA
www.crownhousepublishing.com

British Library Cataloguing-in-Publication Data
A catalogue entry for this book is available
from the British Library.

ISBN 978-184590135-6

LCCN 2008936823

Printed and bound in the UK by
The Cromwell Press Group, Trowbridge Wiltshire

This book is dedicated to my family and friends for their unconditional love of one another

Contents

Acknowledgements

When growing up as part of a huge, extended family I didn't appreciate the inherent values which were embedding themselves into my personality. Saturday afternoons spent with cardboard boxes and foil-covered sticks, fighting aliens and monsters, working in unity as a team in the face of adversity – all were the foundations for the values I developed. Sunday roast dinner spent with grandparents, aunts, uncles, siblings and cousins laid the values of respect, happiness and, on the odd occasion, tolerance. My daughters have inherited this legacy and have an even larger extended family with which to learn and grow.

In 2003 I became head teacher of a primary school in England and was fortunate to work with Bridget Knight and Dr Neil Hawkes introducing *Values Education* into the primary school. I recognised that the aspects and tools they were teaching me through introducing *Values Education* were the same ones I had developed as a child. I would like to thank both Neil and Bridget for encouraging and supporting me on my journey through developing *Values Education*.

I would also like to thank my family, colleagues, friends and the many pupils who have always provided their own insight into how values work in their own lives. My sincere thanks to Caroline, David, Rosalie, Beverley and Tom at Crown House Publishing for their support and advice. Also a huge 'thank you' to my Independent Thinking Ltd associates who energise each other to make a positive difference to the lives of children across the world.

Finally, to Ian Gilbert who has been an inspirational leader and fabulous midwife in delivering this book: I am eternally grateful for your honesty and friendship. The umbilical cord is now cut.

Foreword

What are your values? What are the main principles that guide you in your thoughts and actions? If you are paying a bill at a restaurant and you notice that the waiter has forgotten to charge you for that third crème de menthe frappé do you say nothing and hope he won't notice or do you point it out (in the slim chance that perhaps he'll let you off in return for your honesty, or at least your sense of style)?

Most people have a sense of right and wrong, how and how not to behave. But where do these values come from? And what if mine are different from yours? What if you were to write a list of the values that you felt were most significant? Which would come out on top? What would happen if you were to turn the list upside down?

When you start to think like this, to look at the idea of values more deeply, you start to realise that you carry with you what you could call an ethical DNA – a set of instructions hard-wired into your brain that will determine your behaviours without you even realising it much of the time.

For example – and feel free to try this as an exercise with your friends and family – what if you were to write a list of your top five values and it came out looking something like this:

1. Happiness
2. Love
3. Unity

4. Care

5. Honesty

Such a set of instructions would help create a person who was always keen to look at the bright side of things, always avoided conflict, made sure others were happy and their needs cared for before their own, committed to keeping everyone together and smiling. Sound like someone you know? Your mother maybe? (That's if she's a good one, not one of the evil ones.)

What if you turned the values upside down:

1. Honesty

2. Care

3. Unity

4. Love

5. Happiness

Now you have someone who, above all, will say what they think and expect others to do the same. For them, such honesty shows that they care, even if the truth hurts at times. And can you really love someone if you are not being honest? 'Lies is the opposite of love' as it was once said. Only then can we even start to think about being happy.

Which of the two lists would you want your boss to have? Or your spouse? Or the President of the United States?

You can see how our values are right at the heart of who we are, driving what we do and how we do it. Imagine if you tried on one or two different values for size. How would your life change then? Try a 21-day free trial of a new value and see what happens. Look at Julie's list on page 11 and pick one that isn't currently riding high in your own Top 20 and then try it on for size. 'Courage' maybe? Like Dorothy's cowardly lion, what would happen if you suddenly and consistently were far braver than you had ever been in the past? Would you walk into the head teacher's office and say the professional equivalent of 'Stick 'em up, stick 'em up!'? Or what about 'humility'? How would your relationships change if you spent more time listening to others' achievements than listing yours?

This 'ethical DNA profile' you carry around with you determines so much about your life, but where do the values you believe in come from? As Julie points out, for many of us they are put in place in the family home, from the moment we are born. Where there are dysfunctional families, though, you may get a very different set of values (which is different to having none at all – having no values is a value in itself). This is where school, a good school, can make all the difference to the growing child as a member of a community, as a citizen, as a friend and as an all-round and fully rounded human being.

And this is exactly what *Values Education*, as demonstrated so well in Julie's work and now in this *Little Book*, attempts to do. It helps each adult and child across an entire school to understand, reflect on, think deeply about and become the living embodiment of a series of values that will stand them in remarkably good stead for the rest of their lives. All done in a way that hits so many school targets, ranging from thinking and enterprise skills to speaking, listening and citizenship.

Combining quotes and illustrations from many of her pupils with practical examples and exercises you can try, Julie looks in turn at each of the values she uses across the school year (and it is by no means a definitive list; you may want to use different ones for your own school). The process shows how values can be developed in children at a very young age but not in a didactic 'Thou shalt' and 'Thou shall not' sort of way. We're not talking men with beards and tablets of stone here but a way of exploring human nature and interactions that is powerful and empowering in equal measure.

As a starting point for understanding and using values in your school, this book is all you need. However, one word of caution – walk your talk! We're not just talking about an assembly on a particular value with a parable, a quick hymn and a mention in the school newsletter. You really do have to 'live the dream'. If you spend the month focusing on, let's say 'tolerance', but are the sort of teacher who is quick to explode, to blame, to punish, to shout or to act in any other way that is the embodiment of intolerance then you have a choice (a) you're in the wrong job so go, or (b) practice living the dream and learn how to develop your tolerance level.

So, plan your lessons with care, attend your staff meetings in the spirit of co-operation, eat your lunch with appreciation, write your school policies with simplicity, approach that angry parent with peace in your heart and greet that Ofsted inspector with love.

Ian Gilbert, Suffolk 2009

The Value of Values

The teacher

I have come to the frightening conclusion: I am the decisive element in the classroom. It is my personal approach that creates the climate. It is my mood that makes the weather. As a teacher I possess tremendous power to make a child's life miserable or joyous. I can be a tool of torture or an instrument of inspiration. I can humiliate or humour, hurt or heal. In all situations it is my response that decides whether a crisis will be escalated or de-escalated: a child humanised or dehumanised.

Haim Ginott, 1972

What is your passion?

The first teacher in space was to be Christa McAuliffe. She was part of the seven-man crew on the space shuttle *Challenger*. On 28 January 1986, the flight Christa was so proud to be a part of ended in tragedy when the spacecraft disintegrated over the Atlantic just 73 seconds into the mission.

Christa McAuliffe was selected from 11,000 teachers to be the educational link between space and the children on earth. Her passion lay in education and she encompassed all the values and ideals in which every teacher believes, and although she never got to report from space, she did a lot to inspire a new generation of children to dream

1

about being a part of a future space programme. She also taught us that one of the greatest professions in the world is teaching. I live by her words: 'I touch the future. I teach.'

Do you have a passion in your life – a passion for someone or about something that drives you to pursue it at all times? The word passion has so many connotations, depending on context, but I often wonder how frequently it is used within the world of education.

I am passionate about life and especially my career as a teacher, and now a head teacher. Teaching in the primary sector for 20 years, it was always my desire to make a positive difference to children's lives by valuing them as individuals. It is a privilege to be able to teach and know that you have the capacity to influence the future. Indeed, one of my former pupils is now teaching in the school where I first taught her.

I believe the fundamental quality of being a teacher is to have the passion to value your students so that each and every one of them feels as though they are *your chosen one*. When I recently asked a class of 10 and 11-year-olds what qualities they would find in their dream teacher, these were their answers:

O Is kind
O Is generous
O Listens to you
O Encourages you
O Has faith in you

O   Keeps confidences
O   Likes teaching children
O   Takes time to explain things
O   Helps you when you're stuck
O   Tells you how you are doing
O   Allows you to have your say
O   Doesn't give up on you
O   Cares for you
O   Tells the truth
O   Treats people equally
O   Makes you feel clever
O   Is trendy in clothes and ideas!

Scrutinise this list closely. The word 'teaching' appears only once, in the phrase 'likes teaching children', and there is nothing relating to instructing, but there are plenty of words and phrases associated with feeling valued. If we are going to touch the future and make a positive difference to this planet we all share then, yes, we have to teach children the skills required for them to gain knowledge, but the processes we adopt to deliver that teaching should be based on our principles as human beings. These principles are the universal values we all share, many of which you will find in this *Little Book*.

Reflection task:

Take a few moments to reflect on the word passion *and recognise where it features in your own life. How do you convey that passion? Do you have an icon you admire and respect because of their passion and consequently their actions? How do you let other people know about your passion?*

So what are values? It is values that drive our thinking and behaviour. We behave the way we do because of our internal set of values – our beliefs about ourselves and others that determine our actions, and influence how we behave. This affects the relationships we develop in life and the security we give to others within that relationship.

When I became a head teacher I had not heard about *Values Education*, although I led through applying my own set of values. These, such as love, happiness, respect and care, I had been taught by my parents and family, while others, such as perseverance, understanding, humility and freedom, I had learned through my experiences in life. Today, there is much talk of the breakdown of family values, so where else will children learn such values these days if not at school?

Reflection task:

Take time to capture the values that people who know you would use to describe you as a person. How do others perceive you and what values are present or absent in their minds? Would these values be different depending on the context, e.g. as a work colleague, parent, wife/husband/partner ... ? Be honest with yourself. Are our values always positive traits? I was once asked about the expression of anger and whether it should be considered as a value. Does anger feature as a value in your list and if so how do you deal with it?

Adopting a values-based approach to teaching and learning can radically change relationships, and how the school functions, within a short space of time. It has been encouraging to see how teaching values at my current school, a large primary near Hereford, has impacted on parents and the local community in just two years. It is gratifying to hear the positive feedback from parents telling us how values have had a positive effect on their families and even their own professional lives.

For example, Debs Hiley works as a doctor in the town of Ledbury, Herefordshire. Dr Debs (as she is known) is a parent and now the chair of governors. This, in her own words, is her opinion of *Values Education*:

'When I first heard our new head talk so much about Values Education I was a little cynical. I wondered if it was, as I frequently see in my profession, just another fashion or just *paying lip service to an unattainable ideal. HOWEVER, having spent time understanding how 'values' was to be integrated into every detail of school life by listening to one of the founders of this initiative and seeing how values was a part of every cell of school life, I became the ultimate born-again convert!*

For my children and all the children at Ledbury Primary School I think values aims to instil in them the basic guidelines by which one might hope they live life in a decent, happy and loving manner ... yet aspire to 'be all that they can be'. Sometimes I feel it is religion without any creed or denomination ... a wonderful ideal. But an ideal that is tangible ... And it permeates every aspect of school life so the children truly believe and understand it.

I have seen such changes in children's sense of fairness, justice and sense of responsibility to attain high standards in achieving all their values and a more healthy respect for everybody; this includes both adults and children. In terms of happiness, behaviour and discipline within school I think the impact is enormous. Some of this is quantifiable – for example, exclusion figures have reduced – but much of the impact is immeasurable. Visitors, from new parents to visiting heads, find the 'values' palpable.

Our governing body has incorporated many of the values in its core functioning, especially respect, openness, honesty and quality. We frequently remind ourselves of these values both in the role of day-to-day school functioning but also in the roles we play within school and within our meetings. 'Values' has also helped me to evaluate my life and my relationships with my own family and people I deal with, at school and at work, including colleagues and patients. It has helped me in counselling people at work also; therefore, it is adding to my professional skills.

The 1999 National Curriculum recommended that schools should encompass and promote the enduring values that equip individuals to live in a challenging world. Educators should teach children and students how to value themselves and others. There should be an understanding about developing positive relationships with people living in our families, our communities and the wider world to which we belong. The National Curriculum states, 'Education should also reaffirm our commitment to the virtues of truth, justice, honesty, trust and a sense of duty.'

This element of the National Curriculum is the basis of my philosophy and vision for preparing our children for the world of the future. I believe my passion to engage children in experiencing and learning about values in school will enable these children to grow as resilient people who can successfully embrace this constantly changing world with their own passions.

When I first discovered the work of Dr Neil Hawkes, Bridget Knight, and other colleagues from Oxfordshire, I immediately recognised *Values Education* as a powerful tool to deliver my vision and philosophy, not only as a head teacher but also as a parent. Values have a staged application to living: the values we develop personally influence our attitude to life and can consequently affect others in the world. Ghandi said, 'Be the change you want to see in the world'. Through developing a values-based philosophy, change can happen. How does that work in practice?

Values Education is part of an international and growing movement of educators who believe that, '*Values Education* is a way of conceptualising education that places the search for meaning and purpose at the heart of the educational process. It recognises that the recognition, worth and integrity of all involved in the life and work of the school are central to the creation of a values-based learning community that fosters positive relationships and quality education.'

The Association of Living Values International (ALIVE)

I am part of this movement along with colleagues across Herefordshire and other counties, notably Oxfordshire where West Kidlington Primary School has served as a model for this work. Indeed, some of the powerful tools and guidance you will read about in this book, and most specifically the section relating to values-based assemblies, are attributed to Dr Neil Hawkes (who was a head teacher at West Kidlington) and Bridget Knight.

The *Values Education* approach is an incredibly simple but powerful tool. It comprises discussion about concepts, such as 'peace', 'honesty' and 'co-operation', through assemblies and lessons. It uses periods of quiet reflection, including techniques such as visualisation and the deepening of personal, private and emotionally mature responses to all that school – and the wider world – throws at the children. In this way, children are empowered to take responsibility and become successful in making the right choices regarding their behaviour and actions. These frameworks also help teachers move towards the sophisticated level of participation that is required of them if *Values Education* is to be successful. As Rachel Ussher, a PSHE co-ordinator, says:

> It becomes a part of every day life. The thing about values is that you find yourself thinking about it all the time. It becomes part of your personal life and not just something to be done at school. It makes you challenge the way you and others behave and makes you begin to expect more of your and others' behaviour.

Here is a brief overview of how *Values Education* can be embedded in any school. It contains ideas we have developed with children at our own school (and check out the *Values Toolbox* later on in the book):

- Focus on a different value every month through assemblies and during lessons. Discuss each value at every opportunity and in detail. Within a couple of months children naturally start to use the values language in all kinds of situations both inside and outside school. I smile when parents tell me that their child has told them to become more 'tolerant' at home. The language of values quickly permeates the community.

- Alongside the values, ensure that every adult working at the school who comes into contact with pupils is a good role model for them.

- Consider the environment that staff and pupils are walking into. Look for opportunities to provide a climate of delight and beauty for children to explore;

dedicate special areas for staff and children where they can take time to think and relax.

- Explore teaching *Philosophy for Children* across the school (or *P4C* – more of this later).

- Adopt a positive discipline policy with clearly defined boundaries, consistently applied across the school.

- Involve yourselves in projects that promote team building opportunities, entailing plenty of fun and encourage pupils to take responsibility to organise.

- Implement a 'peer massage' programme from reception upwards.

- Incorporate relaxation and stretching classes in your physical education curriculum.

So, I now invite you to start a journey where you will discover your own values and have time to reflect on how those values affect those around you.

The values explored in this *Little Book* are:

APPRECIATION

Caring

co-operation

Courage

Freedom

Friendship

* HAPPINESS *

Honesty

hope

humility

Love

PATIENCE

PEACE

QUALITY

Respect

Responsibility

Simplicity

thoughtfulness

tolerance

Trust

understanding

unity

The following section details each of these values and how they can be used in your school. I find using selected values for a whole month works well. Everyone contributes to the discussion and people's thoughts are captured and shared via newsletters and the school website, and filter into the community. It will never cease to amaze you how brilliant children are. They come to each value with a very clear idea about the meaning of *that* value relating to their personal context. They will argue and debate the important issues through using their language developed in *Philosophy for Children* and eloquently express their interpretation.

Take time to read each of the values and note how each has been interpreted. This process has taken more than two years and is a result of reflection and discussion. Sometimes you will pick out words and phrases that may relate to a current trend but mostly you will see the underlying themes that we wish to develop and embrace.

Some of the values have anecdotes attached, an example of where it has been clearly highlighted in school life or parents have shared their experiences of values at home. Other values have suggested ideas you may wish to use to explore further. Much of our values work is seen during *Philosophy for Children* sessions. The central feature of a *Philosophy for Children* programme is the *Community of Enquiry* in the classroom, where children are encouraged to talk and listen to each other, and to discuss philosophical ideas. Philosophy enables pupils to develop powers to evaluate and judge adequately and to think critically about what they learn, and this leads to the development of thinking skills. You will read some examples of where *Philosophy for Children* has been used in relation to *Values Education*.

This list is obviously not exhaustive and may alter every time you discuss values, depending on the age, context and experiences of those contributing to the list. The fundamentally important aspect is that everyone has time to stop and think about how these values are used in our every day lives.

The values you choose to explore at your school may be very different to my list. You could have 'resilience', 'determination' or 'enterprise', for example. Choose values that are important to your community; debate and select them, then cherish each one every month; discuss the value of the month at every opportunity and these powerful words will soon become embedded in your school community through actions towards each other.

And, remember, you are living each value throughout the year, NOT just during the month you are focusing on it!

There are contributions from children, aged from 4 to 11, in each detailed examination of the values. You will appreciate the different levels of expressing thinking and language used within each value.

Each value starts with a dictionary definition from the Concise *Oxford English Dictionary*[1]. The values quotes are then taken directly from the discussions.

---

[1] www.askoxford.com/concise

As Megan, aged 10, said: 'Values are not simply words. They are skills we are learning for life and when I grow up I will remember to have them with me and use them to help me live a happy life.'

THE VALUES

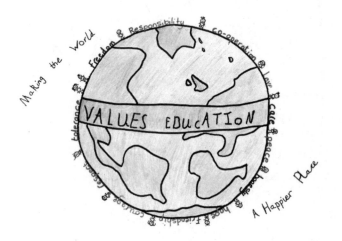

Making the World · Freedom · Responsibility · co-operation · Love · Care · peace · A Happier Place · hope · Friendship · courage · respect · tolerance · VALUES EDUCATION

This boy is appreciating what his friend has given to him

APPRECIATION

appreciation • noun 1 recognition of the value or significance of something. **2** gratitude. **3** a favourable written assessment of a person or their work. **4** increase in monetary value.

This is what the children say appreciation is:

O Showing our gratitude and thanks

O Showing each other that we care

O Being grateful for everything our parents give us; not only presents but their time and love

O Having friendships and co-operating with others

O Valuing other people's ideas

O Thinking about others e.g. neighbours who may need our help

O Holidays and visiting new places

O Respecting everyone for their individual skills and qualities

O Knowing we have clean water, fresh food and clothes every day, unlike some children in our world

O   Being thankful for wildlife and supporting charities like the Born Free Foundation that protects endangered species

O   Having a home

O   Telling our teachers we know how hard they work and that they want the best for us. We will do our best to show our appreciation

O   Knowing that our childhood and education is precious to us and we must value it

O   Living every moment as happily as we can.

Think about who cares for you and all of the people who contribute to your life. How do you show your appreciation? It is often a simple smile, a hug or a word of thanks that is enough to show someone you appreciate them.

Appreciation in action

One of our curricular projects on World War II involves linking our Year 6 pupils with elderly people living in local sheltered accommodation. Once a week the children sit huddled in a small group around one of the elderly residents. The pupils are prepared with questions to ask, such as 'Were there toilets in the Anderson shelter?' and, 'What advice would you give the young people today about "make do and mend"?' The children listen attentively to the stories and anecdotes as though they are experiencing the memories themselves, and record the responses in detail using various media. The old folk are gracious in sharing their memories, forming the basis for a project which engages both age groups in a learning journey and also develops mutual appreciation and understanding across a 70-year age gap which blossoms into friendship based on respect.

These ideas grew out of a wonderful experience I had in my first headship when one of the first incidents of challenging behaviour I had to deal with concerned a Year 4 pupil we shall call Luke. Although he was a boy with huge potential, Luke lacked motivation to learn due to difficult circumstances at home, and was on a cycle of exclusions from school. I worked very hard with Luke, applying the principles of *Values Education*, showing him that someone cared and wanted the best for him and truly believed in him. Eventually Luke settled into a better learning pattern and we also liaised with his parents to help them in developing trusting relationships with each other and their children. In Year 6, Luke became involved in a World War II project that involved visiting elderly members of the community to learn about their experiences. Luke and some of his friends were known as troublemakers in the village where he lived, having been involved in low-level vandalism and disruptive conduct, incurring antisocial behaviour orders, and some of the elderly people were a little intimidated by them. So it was no surprise that they were sceptical about the motives of these particular pupils coming into their homes.

However, the visits went ahead and Luke struck up a special friendship with a naval veteran called Dennis. Every week, memorabilia from World War II would be brought out and shared with the children. Luke listened intently to Dennis' tales of his time in the navy and enjoyed hearing stories about how he had also been a bit of a rogue in his younger days. A friendship developed between the older man and the 11-year-old boy, based on mutual appreciation and respect. The most remarkable aspect of the visits was a corresponding decline in anti-social behaviour in the local community. The police were full of praise for the project and the positive impact it was having.

After ten weeks the children performed a play based on the memories of the elderly community. Each child's part was a character based on the stories of the person they had been working with, so Luke became Dennis on stage. The play was a moving tribute to our local heroes who had given freely of their time and memories to our 11-year-olds, and when Dennis and his friends came to see it there was not one dry eye in the house. The children were rewarded with a standing ovation, and Luke came down from the stage and embraced Dennis, thanking him for helping him to change his behaviour. In return, Dennis presented Luke with a framed photograph of them both. Prior to this project, Dennis had lived all his life in the village, but inspired by Luke's achievements, he declared his intention to visit his sister in Australia. This reflects the power of relationships nurtured through values – all from the starting point of appreciation.

Caring

caring • verb 1 feel concern or interest. 2 feel affection or liking. 3 (**care for/to do**) like to have or be willing to do. 4 (**care for**) look after and provide for the needs of.

This is what the children say caring is:

O Looking after someone new in the class who doesn't speak English

O Helping our friends when they are sad or hurt

O If someone cares for me I feel happy that they are there

O It's important to care for everyone even if it's not easy sometimes

O You need to care about other people to make them care about you

O You need to give care to receive care

O If we didn't learn to care then wars would still be going on

O We care for our school so it is a great place to learn

O Our vegetables grow well in our school garden because we water them and do the weeding

O   It is important to care for yourself. You must wash your body, eat healthily and clean your teeth or they might drop out!

Caring in action

Caring in school

You probably have many examples of how care is already applied in your school, but here are some instances of caring in action in our school.

We have an allotment and the services of a voluntary gardener from our local community who co-ordinates pupil rotas, so the children learn how to grow vegetables and understand how to care for them whilst they grow. It was a super surprise when a group of Year 3 pupils picked raspberries in the first lesson and by lunchtime had proudly placed a warm jar of fresh raspberry jam on my desk! We also have plants and small garden areas outside classrooms and in the school grounds. The pupils care for these areas on a rota system, which means they learn about keeping plants alive.

Volunteers care for younger pupils at playtime and red 'playground buddy' bibs are worn with pride and the pupils enjoy fulfilling this important role.

Our school council is involved in identifying charities to adopt and support. We send shoeboxes filled with Christmas gifts to Romania where we know children will otherwise receive very little at Christmastime.

During 'Healthy Week' pupils write leaflets about caring for themselves.

Teachers caring in their classrooms

One of the most important aspects of *Values Education* in action is role modelling the standard of behaviour you expect from your pupils, and we take time in our classrooms to model care. One of the ways of doing this is to learn something unique about each of the children: do they have any pets or do they enjoy a special hobby? Taking a keen interest in children as people can promote the caring ethos.

Developing thinking about caring

To stimulate interest we use photographs of smart looking palaces and shabby streets, and naturally beautiful places and famous monuments. We then ask the children to place them in order of being cared for, discuss their reasons and challenge their views whilst encouraging them to justify their opinions with examples from their personal experiences.

Caring at home

Sometimes parents complain to teachers that their children are not always caring at home. One solution is to provide the parent and child with a weekly diary. The child is able to self-evaluate how much they have helped to do chores and shown a caring attitude towards their family members. Parents also have to make a judgement. After a week, the diary provides a useful discussion document.

Q: How has *Values Education* helped you?

Values have taught me to be kind to others and to share in my games. I didn't used to come to school every day but I have learnt to respect myself and I value my learning so I come to school more now. I try my best in my work, I listen to my teachers and use my brain.

Jordan, age 11

Co-operation

Co-operation • **verb** **1** work jointly towards the same end. **2** comply with a request.

This is what the children say co-operation is:

O Respect everyone's unique talents and work together as a team

O Work hard to make good friendships

O Concentrate in class so everyone can learn

O Show patience and sometimes tolerance when working in a team

O Work in unity, listen to others and contribute our own ideas

O Show teamwork as a class or group to get things done

O Care for one another so you can co-operate easily

O Take responsibility for your part in the bigger picture

O Know that some people will lead and others will follow

O Listen at all times

O Trust teachers and friends

O Use effort to try your best

O Help your parents by taking on jobs at home
O Value everyone's skills and talents in a team.

Co-operation in action

Once you start introducing values in your school, and talk about them in the community, parents will become aware of the language at home and will happily share with you instances of their children using these values.

Caroline Ainsworth, a parent, describes how caring and co-operation have been key values in her daughters' lives:

I asked my 8-year-old daughter how her work on Values Education had affected life at school. Her initial response was that school had become much more fun. When I probed a little deeper and asked how values had made school fun she explained that because they have discussed how their actions affect the feelings of others around them it makes everyone kinder and more considerate in class and around school. She concluded that values have taught pupils to be more responsible and co-operative and as a result they get many more opportunities to get involved in fun activities.

As a parent with schoolchildren aged 8 and 5, I have noticed that they are more able to discuss issues at home, as Values Education has given them a common vocabulary and understanding, allowing them to express themselves clearly and be understood.

Co-operation

Another benefit is the impact on my children's confidence and self-esteem. They are now more able to assess whether those around them, be they children or adults, are behaving in a reasonable and fair way towards them. I think that this kind of self-knowledge and understanding of those around them will equip them to go out into the world and become more considerate and empowered citizens.

However, a practical example better serves to demonstrate the beauty of Values Education in action. At present my 1-year-old daughter is in the habit of toddling off with my keys. As I was recently tearing round the kitchen searching for them, before our morning walk to school, my 5-year-old patted me on the back and offered to help me look, reminding me, 'Mummy, when we co-operate and all work as a team we can get a lot more done.' I was touched by the wisdom and kindness of one so young and recognised values in both the offer of help and the language with which she expressed herself.

Q: Which value has helped you develop as a person?

Co-operation is the most important value to me because it teaches you to work as a team. Also it helps you to listen which will improve your learning. In our school we play football at playtime but we sort out our problems using our values. Sometimes I need tolerance if someone is winding me up. Being tolerant helps me to keep calm.

Liam, age 11

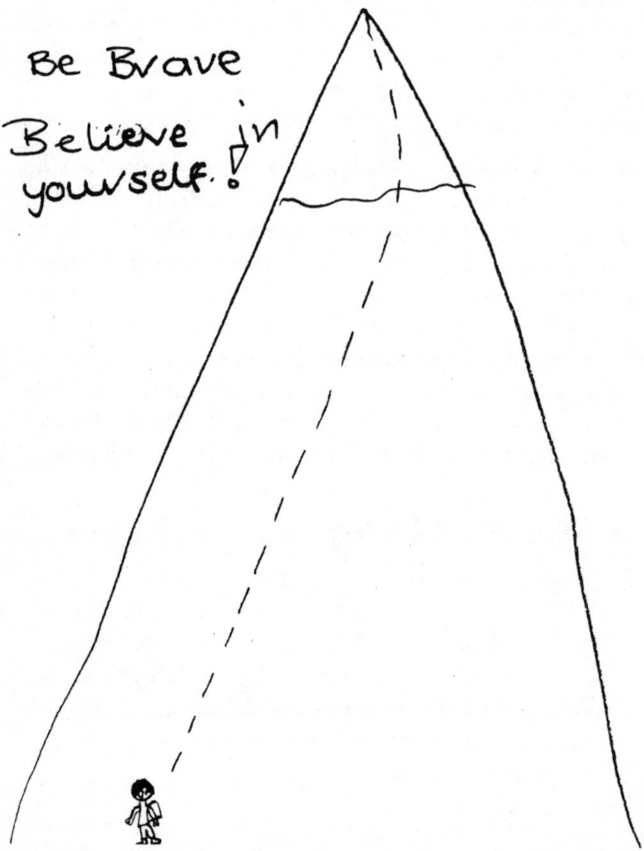
Be Brave
Believe in yourself!

Courage

courage • noun 1 the ability to do something that frightens one. **2** strength in the face of pain or grief.

This is what the children say courage is:

- O Facing your fears
- O Never giving up on something you find challenging
- O Finding the words to ask someone to play with you
- O Standing up for what you know is right, even if you stand alone
- O Encouraging others to do the right thing even if peer pressure is against you
- O Being brave when something scares you, like climbing a high wall or tower at the outdoor education centre
- O Being brave enough to tell the truth even if it will get you into trouble
- O Having the courage to apologise when you know you have done something wrong
- O Having a go at something challenging and giving it your best, even when your fears tell you not to bother

O Pushing your worries aside and GO FOR IT!

O Trying something new

O Rising to a challenge, even if you risk failing

O Being daring, you do stuff other people might not

O Being brave

O Standing up to friends and family if you are being wrongly treated

O Going into the attic without a torch, getting your things and coming back down

O Digging deep to find extra courage to overcome difficulties and challenges.

Courageous children succeed with values!

Curtis, age 11

Courage in action

The following activities can help promote the understanding of courage:

• Discuss when children feel they have been brave. How did they feel inside and what made them overcome any fears?

• Ask them what they can do to build their courage? How can they make what seems to be a scary situation easier to face?

Courage

- Discuss who they can talk to when they need help, both in school and at home.
- Older children can discuss the idea that fear is often just the result of thoughts in their heads (FEAR: False Expectations Appearing Real).

The following projects or activities can reinforce and make courage relevant to pupils' own lives:

- Look at examples of people in history who have shown courage e.g. Martin Luther King.
- Look for heroes relating to a current theme or topic, such as Florence Nightingale, Charlie in *Charlie and the Chocolate Factory*, the children's characters in *The Lion, the Witch and the Wardrobe*, or Harry Potter.
- Ask how people show courage in their local community. How can we help people who are not so brave to develop self-confidence?
- Compare and discuss physical courage and moral courage, asking which is harder to develop.

Q: How has Values Education helped you?

Values have helped me in school not to fight any more. I can use the values to change the world and make it a better place. We help each other in our class, through thick and thin using the values of co-operation and unity. Values makes you more determined to succeed. I use courage to improve my own game.

Corey, age 11

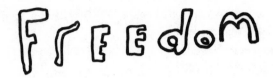

Freedom

freedom • noun 1 the power or right to act, speak, or think freely. **2** the state of being free. **3** (freedom from) exemption or immunity from. **4** unrestricted use of something: the dog had the freedom of the house. **5** a special privilege or right of access.

This is what the children say freedom is:

O You can go where you want to and do what you want to but you still need to think about others

O Not being told what to do all the time

O Giving a friend space when they need time out – don't keep pestering them

O You wouldn't feel happy if you didn't have freedom

O Freedom is natural; spiders have the freedom to do what they want. Before kings and queens and the government, we could do what we wanted to

O Why do animals need to be kept in a zoo? Fish should be released from aquariums

O Feeling happy that I have a school to come to where I can see my friends and that I'm not stuck in the house like other people in the world

O I would like all chickens to be free range to stop them being cooped up

O You need freedom for a full life. Everybody deserves freedom

O Even criminals should get freedom ... but not too much

O We have never had our freedom taken from us so we cannot understand what it can be like without our freedom

O Sometimes it is good to not have too much freedom. You need some boundaries when you are a child so you are safe

O Freedom gives you responsibilities.

Freedom in action

An activity that works well with children aged 8 upwards is to simulate a situation in which a person's freedom is restricted and they are treated differently from other people. Use the example of black people in the United States, highlighting the incident concerning Rosa Parks in 1955. [Warning: I suggest you only do this if you are confident you will not upset the equilibrium of the class, and pre-warn any children with additional needs about the subject matter.]

Rosa Parks was riding home on a bus after work in Montgomery, Alabama, on 1 December 1955. A man got on to the bus and demanded her seat. She quietly refused. The bus driver said, 'If you don't stand up I'm going to call the police.' Rosa Parks replied, 'You may do that.' The police were called and she was arrested and became Prisoner 7053. She was taken to court where she was found guilty of breaking the law, and fined. She also lost her job.

With the United States voting for a black president in 2008, it seems hard to believe that the Rosa Parks incident happened only half a century ago – because she was black and the man was white. The law in the state of Alabama at that time decreed that black people and white people should be segregated. There were separate doors and separate seats on the buses, separate seats in the cinema, separate entrances to buildings, separate park benches. Black people were served last in shops. If a woman wanted to try on a hat, her head was covered with a bag first.

Rosa Parks refused to give up her seat because she was tired – not tired in the sense she needed to sit down, but tired of giving in, standing back, giving way. Tired of being second best, always second best. Beatings and murder on the grounds of colour were not infrequent and black people, whilst enjoying more freedom than their slave ancestors, were still far less free than their white neighbours.

I recommend the following activity to bring home to children the awfulness of this time in our history.

As your children enter in the morning, place blue stickers on one half of the class and red on the other half (or any other colours of your choice). Make sure the 'blue' children are sitting on uncomfortable seats. Be direct with them and give them no rewards. Do the opposite with the 'red' children: praise them, give them fabulous materials to use and allow them to think they are the best. Keep this scenario going and observe what happens. Do not allow the 'blue' children any freedom and discipline them with sanctions for no reason.

The preparation for such an exercise depends upon the nature of the group, and you may want to advise them that they may feel uncomfortable with what is about to happen. Depending on how much support you think the children need, you could give more detail but to keep the drama realistic, the less preparation is better, although children with special needs will need extra support and guidance.

The activity can take place for a whole lesson, with time at the end to discuss how they all felt and for the children to mix with their friends for a 'fun ice-breaker' before going to break.

It could be used as an introduction to other topics such as apartheid or the treatment of Jewish people in the concentration camps in World War II. But if the class teacher feels less confident with the relationships in the class, it may take place later, when the children have a clearer understanding of the subject and are fully aware of why the experiment is taking place.

Although this is a powerful and potentially controversial exercise, the pupils I have worked with have been able to show a deeper level of understanding and empathy in

Freedom

their writing and work as a consequence of participating. And no matter what their response, I promise you will have an interesting debate.

friend • **noun 1** a person with whom one has a bond of mutual affection, typically one exclusive of sexual or family relations. **2** a familiar or helpful thing. **3** a person who supports a particular cause or organization.

This is how the children talk about friendship:

Who are our friends?

O Special people
O People who play with us
O They talk and confide in us
O Stick by us
O People who share and are kind.

How do we show our friends we care?

O Show respect
O Trust each other
O By listening
O Co-operate
O By compromising
O Smiling
O Show loyalty

O Being true
O Always being there.

It's important to make new friends as well as keeping the old. Here are some top tips about being a good friend from a group of 7-year-old children:

O Always keep your promises, don't make them if you can't keep them

O Keep secrets safe, that's why they are secrets!

O Share things with your friends, not just your toys but your ideas too

O Treat your friends the way you want to be treated yourself

O Always tell your friend the truth.

Friendship in action, by parent Anna Perry:

As a parent I was profoundly moved by an example of values in action whilst watching my 6-year-old daughter performing in a whole school talent show. She had chosen to show her diablo skills and was nervous about being able to catch the diablo when she threw it up. She was the first to go on stage and began her routine. I felt nervous for her and was willing her to catch it. Three times she attempted to catch the diablo and missed it each time. The children were with her all the time, in their noises of encouragement and consolation and, as she finished, their genuine applause. It brought tears to my eyes and I was struck by how much respect and care they showed her as one of the youngest performers. The judges (who were four 8-year-old children) made comments which were also extremely positive and afterwards she told me that an 11-year-old boy had come to her and said that he thought she'd done really well and that he couldn't have done it, which she really valued.

Using books to stimulate discussions about friendship is a great way of hooking children into thinking about their own friendships without it being personal. Although many books touch on similar themes, one of the best we use is *The Snail and the Whale* by Julia Donaldson and Axel Scheffler. It is the story of a sea snail that has ambitions to travel and hitches a lift with a whale. Despite his size, it is the snail that saves the whale when he becomes beached on the sand.

By using an outline of the whale, with the snail on his tail, you can brainstorm and display all the qualities shown in the story. Find other stories where smaller animals have helped larger animals succeed. For example, the story in which the mouse frees the elephant from a poacher's net by nibbling through the netting to make a hole eventually big enough for the elephant to break through.

* HAPPINESS *

happy • adjective (**happier**, **happiest**) **1** feeling or showing pleasure or contentment. **2** willing to do something.

This is what the children say happiness is:

O Friends playing together
O Spending quality time with your family
O Freedom to choose
O Playing team games and winning matches
O A big ball of love
O Being star of the day
O Stickers rewarding hard work
O Listening to people laugh
O Making other people happy
O Going to sleep in a warm bed when tired
O Having cuddles
O When someone smiles at you
O Knowing someone cares for you and is kind
O Playing with baby siblings
O Reading a good book
O Holidays in the sun

○ Listening to music
○ Sitting still at the end of assembly, calmly
○ Trying your best to achieve and being praised
○ The first sign of the sun in the morning
○ 'Mum and dad taking me out with my sister for a day's adventure.'

Questions for class discussion: What makes you truly happy? How can we help to make those around us feel happier? What are you doing to help the children in countries where they are so poor but still have smiles on their faces? Do these children need our help if they are already happy?

Happiness in action

One aspect of happiness that we aim to instil through teaching *Values Education* is that it is a state of contentment *from within*. If happiness is sought from outside through, for example, gaining wealth or receiving material possessions, this can only confer temporary happiness. In daily assemblies, children can be shown how to become quiet, still and focused, allowing them time to reflect on the value of the month. This is a precious moment, when the whole school is sitting in silence and taking time to reflect on their own thoughts.

We also offer meditation courses for the children to help them become deeper thinkers. They learn a simple but effective technique called Anapana (awareness of breath) which is designed to help improve concentration and generally gain greater self-understanding and peace of mind. Anapana meditation is not connected to any religion and the technique is an instrument for positive change in behaviour, outlook and well-being. It fits ideally into *Values Education*, giving a practical tool by which children can recognise, experience and practise some of the concepts introduced in school. We have noticed that the children who are able to sit quietly and reflect are often more contented in school and develop a positive outlook on life. The best way to understand how powerful meditation in the classroom can be is to give it a go, so here are my five simple steps to classroom meditation.

This activity is appropriate to teach children from age 8 upwards. Younger children can be encouraged to sit still and be silent as preparation for a more formal meditation.

Five steps to meditation in the classroom

1. Create the atmosphere by turning off the lights and pulling down blinds, closing curtains, etc. You may want to play some calming music very quietly in the background but silence is perfectly acceptable.

2. Either sit children on cushions on the floor or comfortably on chairs. If sitting on chairs, children should sit with their feet placed flat on the floor. Hands should be placed on thighs. No body parts should be crossed. Explain to the children that an important part of keeping ourselves healthy is to have some calm times when we try to relax our minds and

bodies. Tell them that today they are going to learn to be still and silent just by thinking about their breathing.

3. The teacher models the technique and invites the children to join in when they are ready. The following script may be used: 'Sitting very still and silent, close your eyes and focus on the air you are breathing in and out of your nostrils. Just take your normal breathing pattern and be aware of the breath coming from your nostrils. Focus your mind on the area between the top of your upper lip and your nostrils. Every time your mind wanders away try to focus again on this area.'

4. Keep repeating these instructions in a calm voice, reassuring children that they will start to feel relaxed but they need to focus on their normal breathing. After a while the teacher will become silent.

5. To end this time together talk to the children about bringing their thoughts back to the classroom, gently moving their fingers and toes, then other body parts. The children should be asked to open their eyes and stretch their bodies. This is an opportunity to discuss the calming effect on our bodies and encourage pupils to incorporate stillness and silence into their daily routine. Initially the class may manage up to one minute of concentration but this may be extended over time.

Enjoy this time together. The teacher should trust the children to participate by continuing to model this technique. Children with special needs may require extra adult support and some children may opt out initially, but persevere and try to make this a regular practice in your classroom.

Experiencing happy times as a community

Every school has numerous opportunities throughout the year to experience happy occasions. The annual plays, parties and fund - raising events are times when children and adults can relax and enjoy being happy together.

In contrast to peaceful times in school we hold a carnival every June based on a cross-curricular theme which is planned into teaching and learning for the whole week. The most recent themes have been the Wild West and Brazil. Costumes are designed, songs are learned, artists, musicians and others from the local community are encouraged to come and join in. The mayor traditionally leads the procession and declares the carnival spectacular open and the event is a truly colourful and happy occasion for all.

Honesty

honesty • **noun 1** the quality of being honest. **2** a plant with purple or white flowers and round, flat, translucent seed pods, so named from its seed pods, translucency symbolizing lack of deceit.

proverb there are often practical as well as moral reasons for being honest.

This is what the children say honesty is:

O Telling the truth
O Having integrity and using it in every day life
O Being sincere, truthful and trustworthy.

Honest people:

O Tell the truth despite consequences
O Voice opinion in a kind, thoughtful way
O 'Tell on' someone only when necessary
O Show and share their feelings
O Know classmates and teachers care and want the best for them
O Feel and react without guilt
O Express themselves positively as well as critically.

Show your honesty:

O   Thank someone in your family for being honest

O   Tell your parents about a mistake you've made

O   Tell the truth when you've done something wrong

O   Compliment a friend for being honest

O   Express your real feelings without anger, without blaming others, without exaggerating and without hurting the feelings of someone else

O   Turn in something that is lost and encourage others to do the same

O   When someone wants to copy your work, politely explain that it isn't right and that it's best to do your own work

O   Admit a mistake or error in judgement you have made and apologise to anyone it might have affected

O   Do your schoolwork honestly

O   Be truthful with your friends and thank them for being truthful with you

O   When you ask someone to be honest with you, don't get angry with them if their honesty isn't what you wanted to hear.

Honesty in action

The following teacher-led classroom activities for children have proved very successful in promoting the understanding of the value of honesty:

Honesty

- Write and perform a play on the theme 'Honesty is the best policy'.
- Discuss what it means to 'live a lie'.
- Ask the children to list examples of what honesty means to them.
- Debate honesty in sport, posing questions such as, 'Would you be happy if your team won by cheating, such as tricking the referee?'
- Study honesty and dishonesty in advertising. Get them to read or look at advertisements in the news, magazines or on television.
- Help them learn about honesty in scientific or medical research.
- Get them to compare national honesty (crime statistics) with local honesty. Which is higher?
- Research cultures past and present to learn their views on honesty.
- Discuss how the school handles dishonesty. Are there behaviour and discipline guidelines about cheating, stealing, lying and other issues?
- Survey the class to find out how honest everyone is.
- Ask them to collect pictures of people throughout history who have been known for their honesty.
- Get them to write a jingle about honesty or dishonesty.
- Read stories about honesty.
- Ask them to find some quotations about honesty.

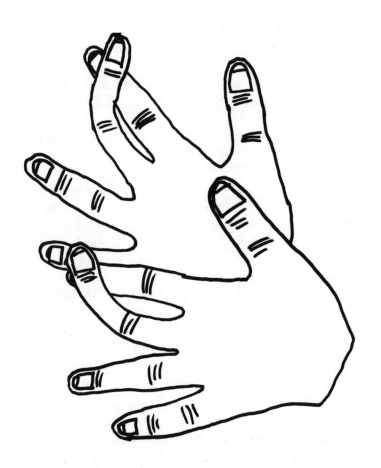

hope • **noun** 1 a feeling of expectation and desire for something to happen. **2** a person or thing that gives cause for hope.

verb 1 expect and want something to happen. **2** intend if possible to do something.

This is what the children say hope is:

- O Believing in your dreams
- O Being determined to get on
- O Thinking of those who have nothing and hoping their lives get better
- O Wanting peace in the world
- O Trying to be friends and getting on
- O Working hard to do your best
- O Not relying on luck
- O Taking time to pray for happy things
- O Feeling someone cares for you
- O Being happy when Father Christmas comes
- O Thinking about what you're doing and hoping to do your best

O You need to be determined to achieve by working hard as well as hoping hard

O Having hope makes you see the bright things in life!

Other words for hope:

O Wish

O Expect

O Faith

O Optimistic

O Desire

What else is hope to your students?

Hope in action

A great story to explore the value of hope is the ancient tale of Pandora's Box. You could use this version below as a stimulus for a *Philosophy for Children*.

At one time the only mortals on the Earth were men. Prometheus had made them, Athene had breathed life into them. The chief god Zeus did not like them.

One day Prometheus was trying to solve a quarrel that was raging between the gods and the men. At a festival the men were going to sacrifice a bull for the first time. They asked him which parts of the bull should be offered to the gods and which should be eaten by men. Prometheus decided to play a trick on Zeus. He killed the bull, skinned it and butchered it. He split it into two portions. In one he put the best, lean meat. In the second he put bones followed by a thick layer of fat. Prometheus offered both to Zeus to take his choice. Zeus looked at both portions, one looked good but was rather on the small side, the other was much larger and covered in a layer of fat which Zeus felt must cover the best, tastiest portion of meat. He chose that one. When Zeus realised that he had been tricked he was furious. He took fire away from man so that they could never cook their meat or feel warm again.

Prometheus reacted immediately by flying to the Isle of Lemnos where he knew the smith Hephaestus had fire. He carried a burning torch back to man. Zeus was enraged. He swore vengeance and started making an evil plan.

Zeus set Hephaestos the task of creating a clay woman with a human voice. Hephaestos worked and worked and created a masterpiece. Athene, goddess of wisdom and Zeus' daughter, liked the clay figure and she breathed life into it. She taught the woman how to weave and clothed her. Aphrodite the goddess of love made her beautiful. The god Hermes taught her to charm and deceive.

Zeus was pleased with what he saw, but he had made her as a trap. He named the woman Pandora and sent her as a gift to Epimetheus. Epimetheus had been warned by his brother Prometheus that he should never accept gifts from Zeus because there would always be a catch. Epimetheus ignored his brother's warning, fell in love with Pandora and married her. Zeus, pleased that his trap was working, gave Pandora a wedding gift of a beautiful box. There was one condition however ... that was that she never opened the box.

For a while they were very happy. Pandora often wondered what was in the box but she was never left alone so she never opened it. Gradually over time she began to wonder more and more what was in the box. She could not understand why someone would send her a box if she could not see what was in it. It became very important to find out what was hidden there.

Finally she could stand it no longer. One day when everyone was out she crept up to the box, took the huge key, fitted it carefully into the lock and turned it. She lifted the lid to peep in but before she realised it the room was filled with terrible things: disease, despair, malice, greed, old age, death, hatred, violence, cruelty and war. She slammed the lid down and turned the key again ... keeping only the spirit of hope inside.

Activities to use after reading the story of Pandora's Box

- Discuss with the children why they think Zeus wanted revenge. How do they feel about the trap Zeus made?
- For older children, why did Zeus choose the terrible things in the box, and can they relate them to what war often brings?
- After local or worldwide disasters have happened people often speak of hope. Ask the children to write a poem or prayer talking about hope for a better world. This may be in conjunction with a current news item.

hope

- A challenging activity is to fill a box with positive words and events. Ask children to write a story in which a box is opened, with positive outcomes.

- In a *Philosophy for Children* session, ask the children the question, 'Can you have too much hope?

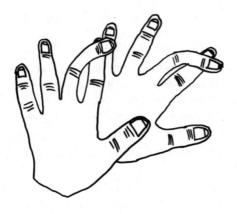

DARE TO DREAM
AND
BELIEVE IN YOUR DREAMS

humility

humility • **noun** a humble view of one's own importance.

This is what the children say humility is:

O I think the American presidential elections are like the tortoise and the hare: the person who is showing off is like the hare and the humble person is like the tortoise and might win the race

O Even though Michael Phelps won eight gold medals in the Olympics, he didn't boast and say 'I'm the best'

O It hurts inside when people boast at you. When I play football and we lose they always say 'you lost' and it's like I've been blown up inside

O It's linked to friendship – if you boast a lot you're not going to get many friends

O If there was no humility then people would always be showing off. This might make other people push themselves too far and it would hurt their emotions

O 'Without humility people might not understand how to be the best they can be.'

This quote came from a 4-year-old boy who seems to have a real understanding of his place in life!

Humility in action

Now that the world is becoming a smaller place because of the World Wide Web, it is possible to enjoy communication and develop friendships with schools across the globe, and many schools find it a very enlightening experience to link with another school in a developing country.

We are linked with Ligula Primary School in Mtwara in Tanzania – a large school with approximately 800 students. When one of our teachers visited it recently, she said it was one of the most humbling experiences she had ever had. The facilities were very poor, with the children being taught in large classes with little or no resources. However, the teacher said she had truly witnessed *Values Education* in action. The students were happy, committed to learning and so appreciative of our teacher's visit, they dedicated a whole day to celebrating her arrival. They had prepared wonderful songs and an English lesson for her to observe, while our school had made a book of photographs, pictures and letters, and we also sent a parachute to teach the students how to play parachute games which the children loved. I think it's important in our possession-driven Western culture that children can see and appreciate how happy some people are with so little.

Another example of the value of humility can be found in the story of *The Tortoise and the Hare*. Through telling the story and acting it out, pupils should be able to identify with the behaviour of both creatures. Older pupils are often able to see themselves in the boastful actions of the hare and reflect on whether they should behave differently the next time they are in a similar situation.

A way of generating humility for a teacher, whilst at the same time judging the impact of one's teaching, is merely to ask the children. At the end of the day, simply asking, 'How did I do today?' can be a very humbling experience indeed ...

L ove

love • **noun** **1** an intense feeling of deep affection. **2** a deep romantic attachment to someone. **3** a great interest and pleasure in something. **4** a person or thing that one loves. **5** (in tennis, squash, etc.) a score of zero, apparently from the phrase *play for love* (i.e. the love of the game, not for money).

This is what the children say love is:

O Being loved can lead you to happiness
O Sharing love gives you joy inside like a big bubble that never bursts, it just keeps growing
O Love is one of the main things we need to exist, along with air and water.

What does it mean if you love someone?

O You put their needs before your own
O You care for them
O You're kind to them
O You want the best for them
O You treat them as you'd wish to be treated
O You show affection to them.

Love

How would you show someone that you love them?

O Give the person hugs and kisses
O Speak to them nicely
O If someone fell over, you could pick them up
O Look in their eyes and smile
O Share with them.

How do you know that someone loves you?

O They smile and look really loving
O They're gentle with you and they always listen.

How does it feel when you know someone loves you?

O Comforting
O Nice
O Encouraging
O You just want to cuddle them
O Warm and happy.

Why is love so powerful?

O When you have love, you have colour in your life
   because when you have colour, it brightens
   everything
O Friends and family are the treasure in your life
   and that's why love is so powerful
O If there was no love in the world, it would be
   dull – everything just black and white

○ Deep down in your heart, you've got to really mean love

○ Love is so powerful because it flows through you all through your life. It starts when you're a baby and you have a lot of love, then when you grow into a child you have a lot of love and respect. You keep growing and keep loving till you're old. Love is like a magnet – it's two-way and keeps attracting.

Love in action

Using the word love in our every day vocabulary is an essential part of *Values Education*. Sadly, some children may only ever hear the word 'love' in school. Look for occasions to use and explore the word. Independent Thinking Associate, Dave Keeling, has started to say 'Love you' to the students as they leave his sessions. (Check out his book *Rocket Up Your Class* for more details.) He says it always makes them smile and often they say 'Love you!' back to him – something quite special with a surly group of disaffected teenagers.

One activity suggested by a teacher colleague that I think is really touching involves making jigsaw hearts for all of the pupils in her class of 9-year-olds. She calls it 'What makes your friend lovable?' The hearts are cut into several pieces and on each table pupils have a piece of heart belonging to each peer they sit with.

Love

Each pupil is encouraged to write a positive comment inside the jigsaw pieces on why they like each person on their table. Each person is given the 'pieces to their heart' to fit together. The outcome should be a positive self-confidence boosting session for all pupils in the class, who all feel loved by their peers.

patience • **noun** **1** the capacity to tolerate delay, trouble, or suffering without becoming angry or upset.

This is what the children say patience is:

O Not losing your temper

O Waiting quietly

O Following the rules

O Being calm

O Controlling your frustration

O Making the right decision e.g. not hitting but walking away

O Being tolerant, especially with younger siblings

O Controlling your excitement e.g. not waking up too early on Christmas Day

O Not interrupting when people are talking

O Waiting your turn

O Builds your ability to be kind

O Being more caring of those around you

O Accepting that people and animals are different

O Finding a way to amuse yourself when you are bored

O Not wanting things now

O Having patience helps you lead a simpler life

O Helps people understand that you can't always get everything you desire.

Patience in action

A great role model to use as an example of patience in action is Nelson Mandela. While serving 27 years in prison for alleged crimes as head of the African National Congress, Mandela came to the conclusion that being patient as he stood up for his beliefs would achieve far greater ends than resorting to fighting.

If you are working with 9 to 11-year-old children, encourage them to think about the value of patience in relation to the life of Mandela and his time in prison. Children can work in pairs to describe him as a person and produce a list of adjectives that best sum up the man who went on to become the first democratically elected president of South Africa and winner of the Nobel Peace Prize.

In a drama-style activity, mark out the size of his cell on the hall floor and then restrict the children individually to that area for a period of time. They should begin to empathise with the degree of patience Mandela demonstrated.

PATIENCE

Children's insights into Mandela's characteristics will be all the more interesting when they draw on their work, exploring values and how they can influence the way we behave in our day-to-day lives. This can provide a great way in to explore the idea of using 'fighting' words in debate, rather than physically hurting someone, leading on to discussions around how Mandela ultimately achieved everything he wanted for South Africa by using words, peaceful actions and patience.

If you are angry you can calm down with a candle

peace • **noun** **1** freedom from disturbance; tranquillity. **2** freedom from or the ending of war. **3** (**the peace**) Christian Church: an action such as a handshake, signifying unity, performed during the Eucharist.

— Phrases **at peace** **1** free from anxiety or distress.

This is what the children say peace is:

O When you don't want to be with anyone else and you just want to have some quiet time

O Countries can be at peace with each other when they're not fighting

O When we sit very still in assembly it is like the world has almost stopped. It is quiet and peaceful

O If you want to be alone you can go into the friendship garden where it is peaceful

O It is one of the most important values because you need peace to not be mean and shout at people

O It helps to calm you down.

Peace in action

One of the most rewarding activities I have observed children engage in is when they are asked to interpret what a value would be like if it were a colour – the most fascinating being for the value of peace. Children have such open views about art and are happy to interpret their ideas through this medium (as long as their work is valued).

Younger children tend to choose their favourite colour to represent peace. This may have been the colour of a favourite toy or piece of clothing. Children between the ages of 7 to 9 select greens and blues but are not sure how to use them. Many children want to use a concrete shape or draw a dove in a blue sky.

The most revealing work for peace I've seen came from a group of 10 and 11-year-olds when two children chose their grey pencils to represent peace. They used their pencils to draw an undulating, never-ending landscape, using hatching and crossed lines to create depth. The results were quite stunning and incredibly peaceful.

Q: Which value has helped you develop as a person?

My favourite value is peace because when you are stressed you can listen to peaceful music and you start to calm down and not be stressed.

Cameron, age 11

QUALITY

quality • noun (pl. **qualities**) **1** the degree of excellence of something as measured against other similar things. **2** general excellence. **3** a distinctive attribute or characteristic.

This is what the children say quality is:

O Working together to get quality work in your books

O Making sure you've got a great team

O Achieving quality can make yourself and others feel good inside

O It's about not giving up on yourself; you need to believe that you can do it

O You need quality to care for the world

O Your teachers want you to have high standards and quality work. They plan good lessons so you can always do your best

O If we think we can, we will do well. We say in our heads and out loud, 'I can and I will'. Our thoughts need to be of a high quality; there is no room for negative words

O We need friends of good quality in our lives. The sort of friends who will stand by you when everything is down.

Quality in action

The following activities are brilliant for promoting the understanding of the value of quality:

- Encourage Assessment for Learning and especially peer marking. Teach your children to look at the work of a peer and give 'two stars and a wish' to improve the work (ie two things that are good about that piece of work and one thing that could be improved).

- Write down some quality remarks to use to praise someone. In my room I have a poster headed '101 Ways to Praise a Child'. Ask your class to make a list of quality praise words or phrases to display on a working wall.

- Make a 'Yellow Pages' of skills for your class, asking each pupil to name one skill they feel proud of. It could be anything from solving maths problems to being able to draw people, or being a great friend. Everyone has a quality to offer and this book could be added to as the year progresses.

- Develop a school achievement award along the lines of the Duke of Edinburgh Award Scheme. I first saw this idea being presented by Chilcote School in Oxfordshire. They designed ten activity areas for their children to participate in. Each area had a bronze, silver and gold level and the children had to complete eight out of ten activities to gain each level. We have developed our own with a values focus.

- Hold a whole school presentation competition when 'Quality' is the Value of the Month. Display pupils' work throughout the school.

- Take time to explore the nature of friendship and what is involved in high quality friendship. (As an example, in a recent assembly a Year 6 boy was asked about friendship. 'To be a real friend you must show humility,' he said. 'Can you tell me why, Dan?' I asked. 'Honour your friends' talents and don't boast about your own, just enjoy having them.' Quite profound for a lad of 10, I thought.)

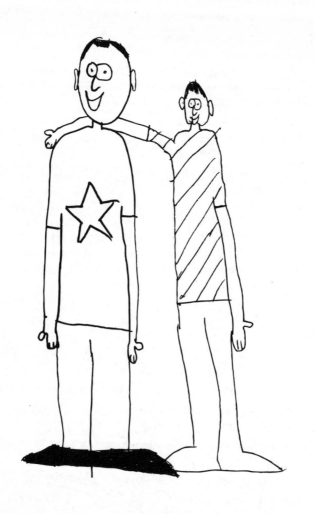

Respect is the key to success without respect you would be a horrible mess this is an important value for you and me.

respect • **noun** **1** a feeling of admiration for someone because of their qualities or achievements. **2** due regard for the feelings or rights of others. **3** (**respects**) polite greetings. **4** a particular aspect, point, or detail.

This is what the children say respect is:

O Caring for other people

O Being kind – be a buddy

O Including everyone in your games

O Valuing other people's ideas

O Loving your family

O Looking after property at home and school

O Respecting everyone for their individual skills and qualities. We are all unique!

O Valuing our education by listening and aspiring to do our best

O Sorting out our problems by talking them through

O Following the football charter

O Think before you speak and treat others as we want to be treated ourselves

O Thinking about the global environment and recycling, re-using and reducing our waste

O Encourage and applaud everyone's ideas

O Looking after ourselves by sleeping, exercising and eating a balanced diet

O When we are angry we can't make the right choices in how we behave

O We need to respect our freedom

O It is good to have someone to lead you who shows respect at all times, someone like Nelson Mandela.

Think about who cares for you and how they show respect towards you. It is often a simple smile, a hug or a word of thanks that is enough to demonstrate to someone you respect them.

Respect in action

The best example I can give you of respect in action comes from the school where I took up my first headship. It concerns a school leaver who really embodied how the understanding of the value 'respect' can impact on a young life in a powerful, long-lasting and life-changing way.

Nine-year-old Debbie was a troubled child with challenging behaviour when *Values Education* was introduced to the school. She was also a bright child with the potential to excel in literacy and acting, and as we discussed a new value each month over two school years, a young, restless and rebellious Debbie transformed into a confident girl who started to take responsibility for herself and her actions.

In the school leavers' assembly for Debbie's year group, the children had decided to choose their favourite value and share their thoughts with the parents and the whole school. The children's thoughts and words were profoundly moving and each child had matured as a result of engaging in *Values Education*. When Debbie stood up we were incredibly proud of her insights when she told everyone:

A couple of years ago I didn't understand the values words. When we learnt about the value of respect the first time I realised how important it was to respect my teachers, my parents, my friends and my work. This time when we thought about respect I realised it is about respecting myself and taking responsibility for the way I am.

She truly embraced the values journey, which had the added benefit of helping her become self-motivated, without needing to search for extrinsic rewards. Debbie has gone on to succeed academically at her high school and perform in a local drama group.

Responsibility

responsibility • **noun** (pl. **responsibilities**) **1** the state or fact of being responsible. **2** the opportunity or ability to act independently and take decisions without authorization. **3** a thing which one is required to do as part of a job, role, or legal obligation.

This is what the children say responsibility is:

- We all have different jobs to do in school
- We are responsible for our own actions
- Respecting your teachers by being responsible for listening and learning in class
- Caring for your possessions and those of other people
- Returning books and toys to their right places
- Help to look after our school e.g. pick up litter
- Helping at home by getting things ready e.g. get uniform
- Being responsible for ourselves by eating healthily, exercising, working hard and enjoying our play
- Thinking about being responsible for our planet; reduce waste and recycle, walk as much as possible

O Being responsible about the world and people who are less fortunate e.g. help the children in Romania by sending Christmas boxes

O Our behaviour is our responsibility. We can learn from our teachers and parents but we make the decisions about how we will behave

O We all have responsibility to make our world a better place. By working together, as a team, this can be achieved

O Looking at our community and seeing what we can do to help other people, such as raising money for projects or assisting the elderly.

Responsibility in action

The majority of classes in schools across the world discuss jobs and areas of responsibility at the start of the academic year but here is an example of what can happen when an entire school embraces responsibility through running a whole school café.

In my experience, when children are empowered through being trusted they are able to take on quite demanding roles and responsibilities. I have seen every class at our school run their own class café for a week of the year as part of the 'Cafe@LPS' (Café at Ledbury Primary School) project. This involved activities including negotiating their various roles and responsibilities with the teacher and becoming true entrepreneurs. One enterprising group of 8-year-olds took photos of their parents on their café day, printed them out on the class computer, and sold them for a quite substantial fee!

Pupils in each year group have to decide on the theme for their café, plan and make products to sell, decide on which pupils are going to fulfil which roles – from chief dishwasher to head waiter. They then calculate which year group made the most takings, and profits are given to the school council, which is responsible for spending the money appropriately.

Q: Which value has helped you develop as a person?

My favourite value is responsibility because thinking of being responsible and being trusted by others makes me feel very happy, whatever the situation.

Daniel, age 11

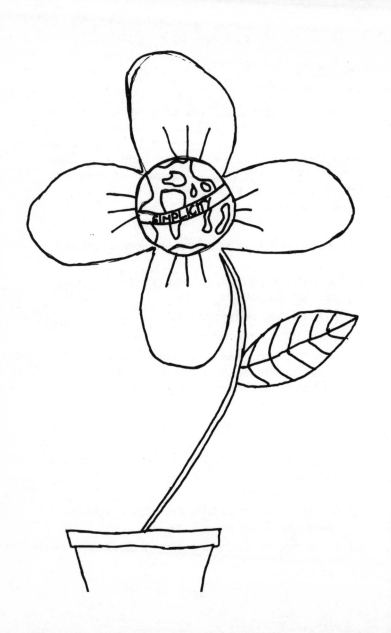

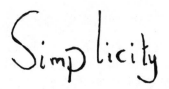

simplicity • noun the quality or condition of being simple.

This is what the children say simplicity is:

O If you didn't have simplicity everyone would be confused

O If you do everything complicated you'll get yourself in a muddle

O It makes you relaxed and calm

O Simplicity is what makes things beautiful

O Nature is simply beautiful. When you see the petals on a flower it can sometimes look complicated and simple at the same time. God must be very clever

O I like giving my mum a hug. She always smiles when that happens

O We enjoy playing simple games in the playground like chasing and skipping. We don't need expensive toys for our games

O Rainbows are simple with their bright colours. I always say 'wow' when I see one

O I like it when lessons aren't too difficult.

Simplicity in action

One of the simplest activities we use for exploring the value of simplicity is one we call (unapologetically) 'Poet-Tree'. It is a simple but effective activity for the whole of the primary age range, it enables the teacher to get the children outside at any time of year and has explicit cross-curricular links.

Take your class outside to explore trees in the school grounds or locality. Encourage them to use their senses (except taste!) to explore the trees. Some questions to stimulate thinking could be:

- What does the bark on the trunk feel like?
- Do the roots remind you of anything?
- Describe the shape/colour/size of the leaves.
- Look up through the leaves, what do you see?
- Can you think of words to compare the parts of the tree to something else? (Children often say the twigs are like 'crooked witches' fingers reaching out'.)

Even just asking them simply to sit still and listen to the rustling of the leaves in the wind can bring all sorts of benefits. Record pupils' ideas either by using a sound recording device or video recorder or with paper and pencil. The activity can also incorporate art activities including sketching and collage.

When you return to the classroom, pupils can collect their ideas to make either individual, group or class poems that collectively are called 'Poet-Tree'. The finished work makes a fantastic display that children, and teachers, can be very proud of.

The simplest things in life are free and fun. I like going down the hill in my go-kart-whee!

Bang! Bang!

thoughtfulness

thoughtful • **adjective** 1 absorbed in or involving thought. 2 showing careful consideration or attention. 3 showing regard for other people.

This is what the children say thoughtfulness is:

O You need to have thoughtfulness to have friends

O A way to show thoughtfulness is to help someone if they have fallen over in the playground

O It is a great value because you think about people other than yourself

O We need to be thoughtful towards people in our community. Sometimes old people can't get out so we could help them by doing their shopping

O You need to be thoughtful at home. You must help keep your bedroom tidy and put your toys away

O I was thoughtful on Mother's Day when I gave my mum some daffodils, it made her smile

O The Good Samaritan was thoughtful. He stopped and helped the man but the others didn't

O Sometimes we act before we think. This can hurt other people so we must stop, think and then react.

Thoughtfulness in action

Thinking of others comes naturally to children who have a values-based approach to life. Many schools either adopt a charity to support or choose different charities throughout the school year. Here are a few examples of charitable events we participate in.

Every year we deliver our harvest gifts to local people as well as collecting dry products and toiletries to send to people abroad. The children also raise a substantial amount of money for different charities throughout the year, and the fund-raising ideas are often initiated by the pupils. Last year a group of 6 and 7-year-old-girls were inspired to raise money to support the education of a street child in Brazil.

They devised a day based on bright colours and selling drinks and refreshments, calling it 'Rainbow Café'. They wrote a letter to the parents explaining their idea, asking for their help on the day. Every child came to school dressed in a colour of the rainbow and paid a donation for the privilege. The 'Rainbow Café' day raised enough money to fund education for two street children and the girls' hard work and thoughtfulness was rewarded when a representative from the charity involved with Brazilian street children came to receive the donation from them in person.

While similar activities are quite common in good primary schools, with *Values Education* you have a real structure to explore in depth and unpick the issues, themes and concepts involved in such acts of charity.

Another way in which focusing on thoughtfulness can be of use is to explore emotions such as anger – an emotion that can cause so much damage and hurt at school. Being mindful of others' needs and putting those before your own can be a hard lesson to learn at any age. Anger can often be caused inadvertently, by ignoring other people's thoughts and feelings for example, and can result in inappropriate actions. It is important we address this emotion. Children need to understand what they can do if their thoughts lead them to feeling angry. Anger can be explored through drama, discussions and role-play, and children should be encouraged to think of what they would do if they find themselves in a difficult situation. By employing the value of thoughtfulness, this can be done in a positive and empowering manner.

Q: How has *Values Education* helped you?

Values are something you should have. Values do not cost anything and could change your life to make it better.

Cameron, age 11

fire   sea

tolerance

tolerance • **noun 1** the ability, willingness, or capacity to tolerate something. **2** an allowable amount of variation of a specified quantity, especially in the dimensions of a machine or part.

This is what the children say tolerance is:

- O Listening to other people's views
- O Showing respect for each other
- O Knowing that different people have different views and valuing that individuality
- O Being kind to each other
- O Showing patience – waiting for your turn
- O Understanding others' needs
- O Co-operation
- O Treating others as you want to be treated yourself
- O Putting up with noise at lunchtime!
- O Trying to get along with brothers or sisters who may sometimes annoy you
- O Standing up for what you believe in
- O Listening and taking advice

O Showing appreciation of everyone's differences

O Understanding that sometimes things go wrong

O Accept that we all make mistakes; we should not blame others when things go wrong.

Tolerance in action

Tolerance is about appreciating that we all have different views and opinions. Sometimes this makes people uncomfortable but through understanding tolerance we can learn how to accept others whilst not always agreeing.

An effective activity is to use a food that pupils will either love or hate. Marmite springs to mind at this point! The children are asked to choose whether they 'love it' or 'hate it'. Using such emotive terms presents children with the opportunity of open debate from the start.

The Marmite question will often separate good friends (not to mention husbands and wives). Once in groups the children have to persuade the opposing team why they should love or hate Marmite. Such a challenge also actively promotes listening skills, debating prowess and understanding.

The point of the activity – and of course you can use other foods or objects, such as pictures of spiders, to provoke similar discussion – is to prove to children that when you hold strong views on a subject, you need to acquire and use persuasive skills to convince someone else to value your opinion. You also need a tremendous amount of tolerance, as it is likely no agreement will ever be reached. Especially about Marmite.

Intolerance is usually rooted in fear of the unknown. Ignorance and fear of other cultures, natures and religions can lead to children developing poor attitudes towards accepting and celebrating an individual's self-worth. So it is imperative that we teach children tolerance and human rights. We should encourage children to be open-minded individuals who are curious and want to learn about others apart from themselves.

We need to challenge stereotypical views of other cultures and religions through establishing global links with our schools. Try asking your children what they would need for a visit to Africa. Do they think there are cities in Africa or safari lands full of animals? What do people live in? Is there running water? These are just some of the questions children ask about Africa and indicate how we need to give a better and clearer picture of other cultures. Constant association of Africa with animals, poverty and exotic behaviour affects the perception of African-American and black heritage around the world. Such deficit images of Africa contribute directly to racism.

Initiate a discussion on the meaning of 'the right to vote'. Teach the children about different periods of history when some citizens around the world were forbidden to vote. Explain why women were not allowed to vote until the start of the last century. What happens in other countries today? Is everyone allowed to vote? Set up a system of voting to make decisions in your classroom. Find out how the school council works.

Develop a class approach to accepting newcomers. Ask the children how they would make a new child, who doesn't speak English, feel welcome. For example, a child called Siebe may not look like any of the other children. Ask how they feel about making friends with someone who dresses 'strangely', who carries him/herself differently, who speaks with an unfamiliar accent or who rarely speaks at all. How will they get to know a new person and understand the differences they may display?

Trust

trust • noun 1 firm belief in the reliability, truth, ability, or strength of someone or something. **2** acceptance of the truth of a statement without evidence or investigation. **3** the state of being responsible for someone or something.

This is what the children say trust is:

What does it mean if you trust someone?

O You know they're responsible enough to do something for you

O You ask someone to do something and you know they'll do it

O They keep their promises

O You believe what they say

O You feel comfortable with them

O Sometimes you have to trust children to do adult jobs.

What would someone have to do to prove they could be trusted?

O Do what they said they would do when they said they would

○ Be sensible
○ Listen well and follow instructions
○ Be true to their word
○ Tell the truth
○ I can be trusted when I don't give in to temptation.

Trust in action

Using the wonderful tool *Philosophy for Children* examine the following quote: 'Trust is like a vase ... once it is broken, though you can fix it, the vase will never be the same.' Asking your children whether they think this is true, or if someone should learn to forgive and trust again, is a great starting point for a very powerful discussion.

Like many of the values, the idea of trust can be used as a way of exploring other topics. For example, in today's society risk and risk taking are huge issues. Every school should carry out activity risk assessments, and sometimes teachers and parents are reluctant to allow the children to participate in activities if there is an element – or a perceived element – of risk. Through the value of trust, teachers and pupils can develop confidence in taking more risks. Alongside trust comes responsibility and once everyone is comfortable that these values have been embedded then roles are clearly delegated and jobs can be completed without fear of things going wrong.

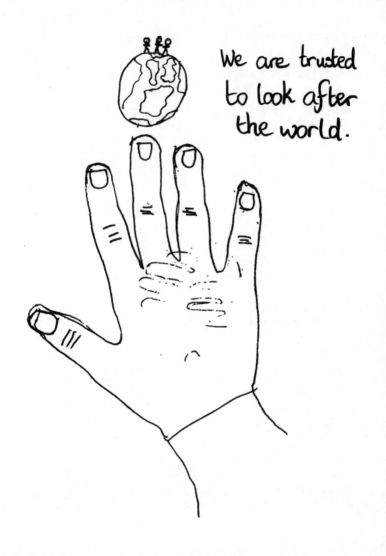

We are trusted
to look after
the world.

Here are some examples of how you can use activities to promote trust:

- At lunchtime allow children to choose where they want to sit in the dining hall. The fewer rules in place, the easier it is to manage lunchtimes which should be a time for relaxation with friends and an opportunity to catch up on the news.

- When children are in the playground trust them to use all available space. In a large primary school, that requires a huge amount of trust.

- Place an attractive bowl filled with beads in a prominent position in school, such as the front of the assembly hall, then choose some of the values – maybe co-operation, tolerance and respect – and put the names on the front of some large jars. When children show these values tell them, and then trust them, to place a bead in the jar reflecting the value they have demonstrated. When one of the jars becomes full the children may select a whole school reward.

- Let the children earn team points for their reward system. Teachers should trust children to record the team points honestly on their personal and class team charts. This then leads to both personal and team rewards.

- Jobs around school can be given to all pupils. These could include putting out chairs, helping to run assemblies and being playground buddies. Increasingly in schools older bilingual children are helping new arrivals, who only speak their mother tongue, to settle in to their new classes.

- Encourage children to take responsibility for running charity days in school.

We are trusted to look after the world.

understanding

understand • **verb** (past and past part. **understood**)
1 perceive the intended meaning of (words, a language, or a speaker). 2 perceive the significance, explanation, or cause of. 3 interpret or view in a particular way. 4 infer from information received. 5 assume that (something) is present or is the case.

This is what the children say understanding is:

○ You need to understand what people are saying if you are going to sort things out

○ If you want to go to the beach but the weather is bad don't get in a strop but understand why you can't go

○ Understanding is knowing when people want you there and sometimes when they don't ... like if they are in a bad mood

○ Some people have disabilities and we need to understand how they look after themselves. Sometimes these people need our help

○ I want to understand how people are feeling. I need to look at their bodies sometimes to see if they are happy

O We must try to understand our teachers but always ask if we want help.

Understanding in action

Using drama is a great way to get children to understand a situation, another person or to feel empathy for a set of circumstances. Using 'freeze frames' in drama you can take a moment from history or a current affairs event or a story that is being discussed in class, to track the thoughts and understanding of your pupils. Ask children to act out characters in a given scenario and tell them to freeze at a crucial point. Now ask how they felt at this point. Their perception will be influenced by the character they are playing.

Here are some examples you could use with children:

- Freeze the story of Pandora's Box just after Pandora opens the lid and ask, 'What did Pandora think?' (See story on page 56).

- Tell the children to imagine they are Little Red Riding Hood skipping through the woods. Freeze at the moment of meeting the wolf. How do they feel?

- Create a World War II Anderson shelter and evacuate children from the classroom into the shelter. Freeze the frame as some children are inside and some outside. Compare and discuss how each group feels. (See activity on page 18).

- Ask the children to imagine they are a figure in a Lowry picture then discuss how Lowry saw each of the figures he drew. Freeze frame the picture ten seconds before or after. Ask if the picture changes.

Book ideas for helping to promote understanding

Lost and Found (Oliver Jeffers; HarperCollins)

One day a boy finds a penguin on his doorstep. It's not until he takes the penguin back to the South Pole that he understands that the penguin wasn't lost, he was lonely.

This is an excellent starting point for considering how we can understand how someone else is feeling, particularly through non-verbal signals. Use a laminated outline of a penguin without a face. Ask the children to draw different expressions onto the penguin.

Giraffes Can't Dance (Giles Andreae; Orchard)

Gerald the giraffe is not a good dancer and dreads the annual Jungle Dance. One night, however, he discovers that we're all different and sometimes all we need is a different song to dance to.

The author wrote this book after a trip to Kenya when he was surprised by how such gangly creatures could move so gracefully. Use this idea to ask the children what gifts they have that others might not be aware of.

FOOTBALL TEAM WORKING TOGETHER!

unity • **noun** (pl. **unities**) **1** the state of being united or forming a whole. **2** a thing forming a complex whole. **3** in mathematics the number one.

This is what the children say unity is:

○ Unity means a shared set of goals

○ We gather together every day in our assemblies

○ Learn our values as a class and school

○ We co-operate to be united

○ We show respect and friendship to each other

○ Unity is seen through team work in our sports teams, music groups e.g. Belle Plates

○ Teachers and other staff all need to work in teams to achieve the best outcome for our school

○ Unity mixes with co-operation (you have to share to shine!)

○ Showing unity is a great way of making friends

○ Unity is about sticking together even when things get tough and we want to give up. We can do it if we help each other.

Unity in action

A wonderful example of unity is to be found in the study of geese, of all things. Children love this idea so, for those of you who don't know it, here is *Lessons from Geese* by Ryugen Fisher, John Lyons and Robert McNeish:

Fact 1: As each goose flaps its wings, it creates uplift for the bird that follows. By flying in a 'V' formation, the whole flock adds 71% greater flying range than if each bird flew alone.

Lesson: People who share a common direction and sense of community can get where they are going quicker and easier because they are travelling on the thrust of one another.

Fact 2: When a goose falls out of formation, it suddenly feels the drag and resistance of flying alone. It quickly moves back into formation to take advantage of the lifting power of the bird immediately in front of it.

Lesson: If we have as much sense as a goose, we should stay in formation with those headed where we want to go, be willing to accept their help and give help to others.

Fact 3: When the lead goose tires, it rotates back into formation and another goose flies to the point position.

Lesson: It pays to take turns doing the hard tasks and sharing leadership. As with geese, people are interdependent on each other's skills, capabilities and unique arrangement of gifts, talents and resources.

Fact 4: The geese flying in formation honk to encourage those up front to keep up their speed.

Lesson: We need to make sure our 'honking' is encouraging. Productivity is much greater in groups where there is encouragement. The power of encouragement (to stand by one's heart or core values and encourage the heart and core of others) is the quality of 'honking' we seek.

Fact 5: When a goose gets sick, wounded or shot down, two geese drop out of formation and follow it down to help and protect it. They stay with it until it dies or is able to fly again. Then they launch out with another formation or catch up with the flock.

Lesson: If we have as much sense as geese, we will stand by each other in difficult times as well as when we are strong.

Q: Which value has helped you develop as a person?

Unity has really helped me as I am now a better team player and I really respect my friends' opinions more. I think it has helped to make me a better listener and this has made me a better leader. I also think no team sport is quite right without co-operation. It is co-operation that keeps a team together, the closer the team the harder they are to beat.

Rhodri, age 11

THE VALUES TOOLBOX

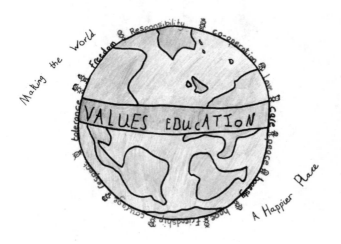

The Values Toolbox

If you have been inspired by the list of values and want to support *Values Education* in your school, here is a set of techniques, tools and activities which have been developed and implemented over a two-year period. Take your time to think about how and when you may use them. The list is not exhaustive and I would love to hear of other tools and techniques you may have developed.

Tool One – Being a role model

If you have one rule only, try ...

'NO SHOUTING'

This applies to everyone, including all staff and volunteers. Think of the last time you lost your temper with someone and you shouted at them. Think about how you felt both physically (red, flushed, tense ...) and emotionally (blood boiling, out of control ...).

Did shouting resolve the situation? Did you gain the person's respect and understanding for your view and opinion? Or is that relationship now strained and tense?

Well here's an idea! Try getting your point across without losing your temper and your poise. No one hears the screaming anyway. Somehow, the message gets lost in the way it's delivered. The truth is it is *you* who is out of control and sending completely the wrong messages to the person you are shouting at. Any mutual respect will be lost and trust misplaced.

Don't believe me? Remember that teacher or boss you once had who thought the right thing to do was to shout at you? As a cautionary tale, here is an incident from my earlier school days, something still I clearly remember:

When I was 7 years old, my class teacher liked shouting. Although I winced when she shouted at my peers because it was not directed at me, I accepted that this was part of her daily ritual. Indeed, when playing 'teachers' in the play-ground with my friends this is what I believed teachers were like. My friends and I would take up the shouting stance if we were playing 'Miss' and shout at the unfortunate 'pupils'. Then one day it was my turn to be shouted at. I cannot recall my mistake or even remember if I had done anything wrong but I must have committed an offence in the eyes of my teacher. What I clearly remember is her hands linked by the wrists behind her back, her large eyes out on stalks as she leaned in towards me with smelly breath, and her shouting at me so loudly that I stood there and lost control of my blad-der. A small steady stream became a puddle at my feet but I refused to cry. I just had an overwhelming feeling of embar-rassment and real hatred for this teacher. From that day onwards I resented every word she spoke and disengaged with learning in her class until I moved up a year and had a kind-hearted male teacher who restored my faith in the teach-ing profession.

Since becoming a head teacher I vowed that I wouldn't allow shouting in any school I led.

So, think of all the things you can do instead of shouting. After all, as Independent Thinking founder Ian Gilbert once said, 'Why do teachers shout at children? Because they can!'

Tool Two – Positive discipline policy

'The most common causes of misbehaviour in the classroom are: boredom, inability to do the work set, being asked to work for too long, not understanding what is expected of them, attention seeking, not feeling valued'

(Additional Needs Net 2002)

Instead of implementing a behaviour and discipline policy based on sanctions consider making it a positive discipline policy with clearly defined boundaries, something that is then consistently applied across the school. Giving children rights and responsibility, which involves them making choices which lead to consequences, is the most powerful vehicle for promoting a positive discipline policy. A school needs rules and routines which are negotiated and agreed by everyone, but trusting children through a values-based philosophy will minimise any potential conflicts which may arise. Whatever age the children are in your class, here are a few basic principles on which teachers agree:

- Learn what is typical for the pupils' age. Many discipline problems happen because teachers expect too much of their pupils. For example, sitting still for long periods of time without a break. As Dr Andrew

Curran says in *The Little Book of Big Stuff about the Brain*, 'You can't be older than your brain!'

- Make sure your lessons are planned but be flexible. Tell your pupils your expectations and desired outcomes, but ensure your planning reflects enough activities to take account of different learning styles and multiple intelligences.

- Be positive and show plenty of praise, either verbally or non-verbally. Be prepared to use sanctions as a last resort and make sure there are stepped consequences. Using the language of values will give you a great range of vocabulary with which to make your point.

- Be consistent, so your pupils will know you mean what you say. Work with your colleagues, especially within your class, so that your pupils get the same messages from all of you.

- Establish good relationships with parents at the school gate at the beginning or end of the day. Promote the partnership between home and school. Speak to parents about children's behaviour at home. Is there anything you should be aware of which may affect their behaviour in school?

- If any of your pupils misbehave, try to understand *why*. What need is not being met? How could you address that need in an acceptable way?

- Give your pupils choices but make sure either choice is related to the desired outcome.

- Avoid threats and ultimatums.

- Never bribe or make promises you can't keep. Children do not need elaborate rewards for being good. However, Jenny Mosley's suggestion of using 'Golden Time' on a Friday afternoon works well in any school (more information is available on www.circle-time.co.uk).

- Accept mistakes and help your pupils to learn from them. Talk through each scenario and ask the pupils what they would do differently next time. Encourage the pupils to use the values vocabulary.

- To teach children respect, talk to them respectfully – without ridicule, sarcasm, name-calling or humiliation. Be a positive role model for your pupils – it is the most powerful form of teaching.

This is what other teachers and children say about the power of *Values Education* as a basis for developing positive relationships which leads to appropriate behaviour and a happy school.

A 10-year-old girl's view ...

In school my favourite values are respect and co-operation because everyone gets on better. The teachers are good because they aren't moany and picky all the time. I enjoy helping.

The teacher's views ...

Let our love grow in our community and across the world so EVERYONE co-operates to make our planet a happy place to be.

There is no 'I' in the word team.

Values and especially the value of peace has made me calmer as a teacher. This has made my class a more peaceful and enjoyable environment. The pupils respond positively when discussing values and this up-beat attitude improves their learning. This has made a real difference to my classroom.

Values at our school has made an even bigger difference than I expected. It really has turned our world upside down. In two years, as a teacher, I have changed from being a controller of poor behaviour and low-level disruption to being a facilitator of good quality education. It has tipped the balance in terms of making teaching an enjoyable experience for me. I think the change has come about because values gives adults and children alike a new vocabulary and a new space for discussion. In the past, when I have talked to children about respect, they have looked at me blankly and then carried on as before. Now, when respect is mentioned there is recognition in their eyes and a shared understanding of what it means to respect someone or something. I firmly believe that if today's children took their values forward with them into adulthood, the world really would be a different place.

If you have any doubts about introducing *Values Education*, here are the views of a deputy head teacher of a large 3-11 age group primary school:

The children readily took to the promotion of Values Education and were quick to adopt the language, once the values were introduced in assemblies and reinforced by the class teachers.

The children soon began to understand and internalise the values they were introduced to and were keen to demonstrate them as they realised that they would enable them to enjoy school and gave them a sense of 'doing the right thing' which helped promote their self-esteem. They began to notice when certain values were shown by their peers and by adults. The system of individual and whole school celebration of values in practice promoted a sense of well-being, of feeling valued and able to make a positive contribution to the school community. This led to the promotion of a family atmosphere, despite the size of the school, where respect and consistency of message developed a secure and positive atmosphere.

Children have an ability to feel for others once they are shown the value by those around them. The no shouting and the atmosphere developed by the value-based interaction they witness between all staff is important in modelling how to treat and respond in a value-based manner.

This has a positive impact on behaviour as children are equipped with the language to articulate what they are experiencing and can see the other child's point of view by understanding how their actions impact on others. This has led pupils to a greater desire to show self-discipline and enjoy their time at school.

Tool Three – Creating the optimum learning environment

Provide a climate of delight and beauty for both adults and children to enable them to feel relaxed and valued. There should be dedicated areas for staff and children where they can take time to think and relax. A stimulating environment makes for a stimulated child (and staff). This may seem obvious, but it cannot be emphasised enough. Educational psychologists have found that environment can have a huge impact on a child's learning. There are schools and classrooms that alienate children and those that engage them, and much of the research shows that children who feel engaged by their environment are more receptive.

Here are some suggestions about improving the school and the classroom:

- Place plants around the school, indoors and outdoors – it involves the children in having to care for them.

- De-clutter areas on a regular basis (this could be daily or weekly). Involve staff and children in doing this in a designated time period at first and then it will soon become part of the make-up of the school.

- Ensure the furniture in the classroom is appropriate for the age of the children you are teaching. If furniture and classroom elements are thoughtfully considered for a child's scale, children will feel engaged and are likely to have a more positive learning attitude.

- Use your display space effectively. Children feel incredibly valued when they see their work celebrated on display. If the learning environment gives meaningful messages about being cared for, and children feel as though they have ownership on the elements of displays, they will be loyal to their teacher and their self-esteem will rise. You can also use the classroom walls as a learning tool where connectives, number lines and 'wow!' words are made accessible to children. A space can also be reserved on display walls for exhibiting material that relates to the weekly lesson. This can reinforce the lesson and keep the display current and interesting.

- If children can look out of windows, reach storage areas and sit at tables and chairs that suit them, they will feel more involved, more responsible and more confident in their ability to learn.

- Consider the lighting in your room. Try placing table lamps around the classroom and switching off the harsh strip lights and then notice the difference.

- What is the colour of your school walls? What impact does that colour have on people's moods? Our school is painted in a calm aqua frost colour, which we find to be very calming.

- Encourage all adults and children to reflect on the atmosphere they are creating by simply smiling! It is contagious and can change the feel of the whole school.

- Use music to create atmosphere in assemblies and lessons.

Tool Four – Helping children to experience calmness, mutual respect and relaxation through peer massage

The Massage in Schools Programme is an inclusive pro-gramme of positive touch and clothed peer massage. It originated in Sweden and is now being used by schools in Britain. Children wear their normal school clothes and give massage to each other on the back, head and arms. They take part in 10 to 15 minutes massage daily.

Studies have shown that, when children give massage to each other, they become calmer, concentrate better and have more confidence. They learn to respect themselves and other children. Each child gives permission for the massage to take place. If children do not want to give or receive massage they sit and watch.

The class teacher may observe the children before the programme starts and then at intervals to monitor the effect of massage on individual children and the whole group. Parents can help to make teachers aware of changes in their child at home by completing an observa-tion sheet before massage begins and at other intervals. Parents can let the teacher know if they notice anything of particular interest.

Peer massage has had a profoundly positive effect on relationships between children in our school as well as aiding concentration in lessons.

Sara Valve, Massage in Schools instructor, says:

I teach the children how to give and receive a child-to-child massage. The Massage in Schools Programme has been designed for children aged between 4 and 12 years of age to help reduce children's stress levels, improve emotional health and develop respect for the needs and feelings of others. It encourages visualisation, kinaesthetic learning and creativity, as children are encouraged to create and perform their own massage stories related to a current curriculum topic.

An important part of peer massage is that before the massage starts the children ask their partner, 'Please can I massage you?' If their partner says 'no' then that answer must be respected and the pair remains together, but perform the massage strokes in the air. At the end of the massage the child that has given the massage says 'Thank you' to their partner and they swap over. If there is a stroke that the child feels uncomfortable with, then they can tell their partner and 'still rest' (hands held on shoulders) can be used until they are ready to join in again. These rules help the children to feel in control and allow them to make choices.

During peer massage the children remain fully clothed and the massage strokes are carried out on the children's backs, arms, hands and head. The children either sit on the floor or on chairs to do their massage and the sessions take between 10 to 15 minutes. Music is played to help maintain a rhythm and add a calming atmosphere. The first massage the children learn is called the Weather Massage and this is followed by a series of 15, named strokes, such as Eyeglasses,

Hairdresser or Bear Walk and these strokes create the Formal Massage.

It is important to note that the Formal Massage strokes are unchanging in their delivery and order. The rules for the massage are simple, yet they are the very essence of the whole philosophy of peer massage. This in turn gives the children a safe and secure environment in which to give and receive a massage.

During regular peer massage sessions I have observed children, who have shown low self-esteem and are unsure of being touched, grow in confidence, and restless children discover stillness. Class friendships have broadened, as the children are regularly given different massage partners to work with. This connecting, sharing, calming experience helps break down any barriers or divisions which may be present, thus giving unity to the class.

As the children often practise the massage on members of their family, I have seen positive links between home and school develop as a direct result of peer massage.

I believe that, regardless of age, positive, caring physical touch is an important part of our daily lives and vital for our well-being. If, through a short, fun, nurturing peer massage, children can learn how it feels to be calm and relaxed, then an important life skill has been learnt.

Tool Five – Philosophy for Children (P4C)

As already described in the Values section, *Philosophy for Children* is a powerful learning tool that promotes open debate and a depth of thinking rarely seen in a primary school classroom, taking into account all the pressures of today's curriculum. Each session is pupil-led, allowing the children to dictate the course of their discussion, whilst the teachers act as facilitators. The philosophy lessons allow open-ended discussion in which it is the child's contribution that counts. This means there are never any specific right or wrong answers and the children can debate any issue without fear of being ridiculed for saying the wrong thing. Therefore, pupils learn how to listen and appreciate that everyone may have different views, whilst not always agreeing with each other.

The positive impact of P4C lessons can be seen in children's ability to articulate their thoughts more clearly in their lessons. Children take time to reason, express and justify their thoughts using the most appropriate vocabulary. They display patience and respect towards each other as they listen to and value each other's opinions without necessarily agreeing. Children are also able to resolve their own conflicts, as the lessons provide the pupils with both the vocabulary and thought processes to talk over any confrontation without resorting to insults or fighting.

Children, even at a very early age, have the capacity to think for themselves. They bring with them into the class a whole host of knowledge and experience that, if utilised, can speed up the learning process. Philosophy can help pupils make connections between areas of experience, knowledge and learning. Try observing the youngest children in your school as they express their thoughts resulting from each new experience. These children are developing philosophical thinking from a very young age. Nurture and encourage this thinking, allowing children time to explain their thinking fully.

Rachel Ussher is a Level 1 P4C practitioner and has taught many lessons across the 4-11 age range. This is her experience:

Values Education *fits perfectly with Philosophy for Children. The thing I love about P4C is that it is all about the children; from an initial stimulus they decide where the enquiry is going and what the ground rules should be. P4C gives children the freedom to share their thoughts without the fear of 'getting it wrong'. Children who find it hard to accept others' opinions become more accepting; children become more confident to speak; they learn not just to tolerate each other but to respect one another also. Children at our school have had an easier start in P4C than some, perhaps, because they already have much of the language needed to share ideas and also to challenge them because of* Values Education.

Here are a few P4C ideas based on values:

- Do all values have an opposite? Display a list of values and discuss in groups. What does that opposite tell you about the value?

- Honesty: Are all lies bad? When you tell someone their new haircut looks lovely, even when you don't think so, is that acceptable? When you lie about a surprise birthday party, are you, in fact, lying?

- Discuss:

  1. Power or Pleasure?

  2. Wealth or Friendship?

  3. Intelligence or Courage?

  4. Security or Fame?

  5. Freedom or Fairness?

  6. Truth or Happiness?

  Put each pair on a card, one per group. Allow time for group discussions then report back to the group before formulating questions.

- What is the best example of simplicity you have experienced?

- How far would you go for a friend?

- Can we truly appreciate our freedom if we have always had freedom?

Ian Gilbert's *Little Book of Thunks* contains lots of useful stimulus questions.

Tool Six – Stretching and relaxation classes

Values Education is also about teaching children to become self-aware and aware of others. The spiritual world of the child, the inner world of thoughts and feelings, should be nourished and given opportunities to develop. Alongside giving daily opportunities for stillness and calm during assemblies and in lessons, children can also experience stretching and relaxation classes as part of their physical education curriculum. This helps to give children a sense of peace, centredness and self-confidence. It also helps to strengthen their core muscles.

In our school these classes are taught by a qualified teacher of children's yoga. We teach the children a tool to help them live a happy, healthy life. Lessons are filled with fun stretching and moving games interlaced with delightful stories and a quiet time. The teacher leads the children through a series of poses, actions, sequences and balances. The movements can help increase a child's self-awareness, build self-esteem and strengthen their bodies.

Tool Seven – Assemblies

Assembly is when you go into the hall with your clothes on.

Alfie, aged 4

The school assembly is central to the development of *Values Education*. It has a tremendous potential to nurture a positive school ethos that emphasises care and the pursuit of excellence. This helps the school to develop a sense of harmony.

Assembly is crucial to the success of *Values Education*. Having a daily opportunity for staff and children to gather in one shared space and unite in growing together as a school is essential to making values-based schools successful. In a larger school some of these assemblies may take place in age groups during the week but, if you have the space, at least two assemblies a week should bring the whole school together.

The purpose of the assembly is:

- To help individuals think about personal, social, moral and spiritual values and how they might demonstrate these through their words and actions.
- To deepen motivation, responsibility and ability in making positive personal and social choices.
- To encourage educators to regard education as providing students with a philosophy of living which will help them to live lives with respect, confidence and purpose.

Children respond positively to the expectation that the procedure is always the same in assembly:

- The hall should be prepared prior to the children entering. The lighting should be dim with appropriate music playing.
- There may be a table with a lit candle and/or a stimulus to be used in the assembly.

- The assembly leader sits still at the front of the hall next to the table and models the silence and stillness expected from the children.

- Children are led from their classrooms in silence, thinking about the value of the month. They enter the hall quietly and gently. Children sit in a place without being shown by their teacher.

- The assembly leader makes eye contact as greeting with all who come in.

- The leader continues to model the expected behaviour; the adults follow this lead.

- Children are not reprimanded if they speak or move, they are simply expected to quietly focus.

- The assembly leader will greet the children with a positive comment once everyone is in and the assembly theme will be related to the value of the month.

- After singing and a period of reflection, stillness and calmness may follow. Pupils are taught how to sit in a still, relaxed, alert and comfortable manner.

- Pupils gradually develop the skill to withdraw within themselves and use the inner life of the imagination.

- With the whole school sitting silently it is a powerful moment and this may just be the one calm time in the day for everyone.

- Teachers will lead their classes from the assembly hall in silence in preparation for the learning that takes place next.

Leading a values-based assembly is incredibly rewarding and humbling. I have found that this time is a very special start to my day and the peace often remains with me for the rest of the day ahead.

The journey you have been through in this *Little Book* provides a glimpse of how a values-based school in action can look. As educators, many of you may have these values embedded in your philosophy for learning and teaching but are they explicit in the lives of your pupils? And what about in your own life both in and outside school?

So where do you start? Here are a few suggestions:

- Ask the adults in your school about their values and how they make these explicit in their relationships in school.

- Audit where the values are working already and discuss what is different about this class/teacher/area of school. Decide core values together.

- Launch *Values Education* at the start of a term or school year. The first value to implement could be 'Respect'. Adults and children will be able to discuss it openly with children. Start with an assembly where the theme is respect.

- Make *Values Education* displays around the school. Use children's work and words to reflect and celebrate a values-based environment.

- Tell parents about them through a newsletter.

- Talk about them with all adults, especially staff, parents and governors.

- Introduce reflection times and *Philosophy for Children* lessons.
- Incorporate into teaching and learning opportunities.
- Keep thinking and talking about it!

When you develop your values-based classroom or school you may start with using the principles outlined here but inevitably your personality and experiences will provide more tools for you to share with adults and children. How will you know it is working? Well here are a few 'performance indicators' found in successful values-based schools:

- There are high expectations and clear boundaries: the foundations of good values require good discipline.
- The aim is for a calm, reflective atmosphere.
- It is philosophy for children but is enhanced by action.
- Opportunities to discuss values are taken as they arise: they permeate all areas and aspects of school life.
- Teachers remember to 'live the values'. We teach best by being role models.
- It encourages pupils to want to be good citizens rather than relying on 'managing' them into good behaviour.
- Ultimately it makes a teacher's job in the classroom easier.
- It can lead to raised standards in both teaching and learning.

• The school is a happy place to be.

Please let me know about your work, how you introduce *Values Education* in your school and how you get on. You can e-mail me through Independent Thinking on julie.duckworth@independentthinking.co.uk. I do hope you feel inspired to write and tell me about your journey through *Values Education*.

And finally, a poem for every parent and teacher:

A POEM ABOUT TRUST

Trust is what you gain and show
Rely on people you trust and know
Use it to help many others
Show it to friends, sisters and brothers
Trust is to be gained; don't abuse it simply use it!

Poppy, Emily and Anna, all aged 11

We are trusted to look after the world.

Bibliography

Andreae, G. (2008) *Giraffes Can't Dance,* London: Orchard

Curran, A. (2007) *The Little Book of Big Stuff About the Brain,* Carmarthen: Crown House Publishing

Drifte, C. (2004) *Encouraging Positive Behaviour in the Early Years: A Practical Guide,* London: Paul Chapman Educational Publishing

Farrer, F. and Hawkes, N. (2000) *A Quiet Revolution: Encouraging Positive Values in Our Children,* London: Rider

Farrer, F. (2005) *A Quiet Revolution Edition 11: Encouraging and Sharing Positive Values with Children,* England: FH Books

Gilbert, I. (2002) *Essential Motivation in the Classroom,* London: RoutledgeFalmer

Gilbert, I. (2007) *The Little Book of Thunks: 260 Questions to Make Your Brain Go Ouch!,* Carmarthen: Crown House Publishing

Ginott, H. G. (199) *Teacher and Child: A book for parents and teachers,* New York: Collier

Hawkes, N. (2003) *How to Inspire and Develop Positive Values in Your Classroom,* Cambridge: London Development Agency

Hawkes, N. (2008) *The Values Education Folder,* Abingdon: Abbey Press Group

Jeffers, O. (2006) *Lost and Found,* London: HarperCollins

Lipkin, M. (2004) *On Fire! The Art of Personal Consistency,* Ontario: Environics/Lipkin

Loomans, D. (2002) *100 Ways to Build Self-Esteem and Teach Values,* New York: MJF Books

Sharma, R. (2004) *The Monk Who Sold His Ferrari,* London: Element Books

Tolle, E. (2001) *The Power of Now: A Guide to Spiritual Enlightenment,* London: Hodder/Mobius

Praise for *The Little Book of Values*

"Julie has captured something very special here: By giving children the skills to understand what matters to themselves, to others and to our communities through values in this way, she creates a sense of inner confidence that can only lead to them becoming more resilient adults, brilliantly well placed to build purposeful relationships and to face whatever life throws at them. Values Education has the power to transform schools, their staff, children and culture. Julie shows us how."

Rachel McGill, Director, Sunray7

"Sometimes you meet a book which you can't put down, which reminds you of what education is all about and inspires you to want to make a difference in the lives of children. The Little Book of Values is one of those books. It's a humbling and impressive read combining quotes from children with advice for teachers; ideas for assemblies with values that get to the core of what we should be doing in Education. The chapter on 'Honesty' should be compulsory reading for everyone and I will certainly see geese in a different light after reading about 'Unity'. If every child and adult in our community shared these values our world would be a better place."

Denise Strutt, Headteacher,
Whitecross Hereford: High School and Specialist Sports College

"Just buy this. I mean, don't wait – buy it. It's just great. And better than that don't only buy it, read it. But read it carefully. And then stop and think first – how much of this do I apply to myself? And when you have really thought about that get on and do it. Don't wait. The book is full of things to do to make its message a reality. The message? Think of other people. Think of other people intelligently. Especially think of yourself intelligently. You couldn't act on this book and not do that. It is compelling. Fascinating. Gorgeous. All the strong words. It is a book that gives a structured way to help children learn what so much of society has forgotten - its not all about you. Lots of it is about other people and how your actions affect them. Wow. BUY IT - AND USE IT!"

Dr Andrew Curran, Paediatric Neurologist and author of
The Little Book of Big Stuff About the Brain

"A must for every school – order it now! This is because *The Little Book of Values* truly reflects the outstanding Values Education that I see in action at Ledbury Primary School in Herefordshire. This is a wonderful example of a school that 'walks the talk' of Values Education. Julie Duckworth's little book, with an enormous heart, will be a source of inspiration and practical ideas for schools to be values-based communities – a must for the 21st Century. My vision for Julie's superb book is that it will be seen as a vital resource for all schools. Brilliant!"

Dr Neil Hawkes, International Education Consultant for
Values-based Education www.values-education.com

"I remember Julie Duckworth commenting that Ghandi said "be the change that you want to see in the world" - and this underpins her values based curriculum. She believes in giving children the skills they need for life, developing and practising honesty and trust in order that they become responsive citizens.

"Julie's school is a microcosm of her vision for tomorrow's society - one where people are responsible for their actions and for all their learning. It is clear from her book that the ripples from her values based school are already moving from her pupils into their families and immediate environment.

"If our children haven't got the attributes of perseverance, resilience and a positive attitude to embrace the challenges ahead of them - then how can they grow up to be the citizens of the future? *The Little Book of Values* documents the analysis and practice of these attributes in a vibrant school community."

Anne Evans OBE, Chief Executive, HTI

"Values Education is at the heart of many of our schools in Herefordshire, and the quality of their personal development and wellbeing is a testament to this practice and to the individuals who embody it. This book is a celebration of the work at Ledbury Primary School and exemplifies the power of Values Education in transforming schools, and transforming lives. This is a practical demonstration of how Values Education reaches out and touches children and adults alike, enabling individuals and organisations to develop positive strength and purpose through living values-filled lives. Enjoy this book as an uplifting read, or as a toolkit for school transformation!"

Bridget Knight, Herefordshire Local Authority

More Little Books ...

The Book of Thunks: Is not going fishing a hobby?
and other possibly impossible questions to stretch
your brain and annoy your friends
by Ian Gilbert ISBN: 9781845900922

The Little Book of Thunks: 260 questions to make
your brain go ouch!
by Ian Gilbert ISBN: 9781845900625

Little Owl`s Book of Thinking
by Ian Gilbert ISBN: 9781904424352

The Little Book of Big Stuff About the Brain: The
true story of your amazing brain
by Andrew Curran edited by Ian Gilbert
ISBN: 9781845900854

The Little Book of Music for the Classroom:
Using Music to Improve Memory, Motivation,
Learning and Creativity
by Nina Jackson edited by Ian Gilbert
ISBN: 9781845900915

The Little Book of Inspirational Teaching Activities:
Bringing NLP into the Classroom
by David Hodgson edited by Ian Gilbert
ISBN: 9781845901363

The Little Book of Charisma:
Applying the Art and Science of Charisma
by David Hodgson edited by Ian Gilbert
ISBN: 978-184590293-3